# Mastering Docker

## The Ultimate Guide to Seamless Software Development

Nathanial Jameson

# TABLE OF CONTENTS

# INTRODUCTION

Flexibility and efficiency are key components in the dynamic field of software development. There is a growing need for a solution that makes the process of deploying applications across different settings easier for developers, as many struggle with this. Let me introduce you to Docker, a revolutionary platform completely changing how we design, create, and distribute software.

"Build once, run anywhere" is a dream realized with Docker, which solves the age-old issue of "it works on my machine." Docker ensures that applications run consistently anywhere they are deployed by utilizing containerization. However, what is containerization exactly? What distinguishes Docker from conventional virtualization techniques? More significantly, how can you use it to improve the effectiveness of your software development processes?

Designed to be your all-in-one guide to this revolutionary technology, "Mastering Docker: The Ultimate Guide to Seamless Software Development" This e-book offers helpful insights for every step of your Docker journey, whether you're a seasoned developer looking to streamline your workflows or a total beginner attempting to grasp the fundamentals.

We'll go in-depth into Docker's architecture, examine best practices for managing containers and creating images, and even touch on more complex subjects like Docker's role in DevOps and how it works well with Kubernetes. We will also provide case studies from the real world that demonstrate how companies across the globe are using Docker to achieve unmatched efficiency.

You will have a firm grasp of Docker's foundations, its role in contemporary software creation, and the expertise needed to effectively incorporate Docker into your own projects by the time you finish this e-book. Now, let's get out on this journey together to utilize Docker for seamless software development fully.

# CHAPTER I

# Understanding Containers

## The concept of containers vs. virtual machines

Over the last decade, two ideas have been increasingly prominent in the fields of software deployment and system architecture: virtual machines (VMs) and containers. They appear to have the same objective at first glance: separating applications and their environments to guarantee consistency throughout various platforms and systems. They each have different underlying philosophies and methods for achieving this goal, which has different implications for system administrators, developers, and organizations as a whole.

For a long time, virtual machines have been essential to the deployment and development of software. A virtual machine (VM), which is based on the idea of hardware virtualization, simulates a fully functional computer, including its operating system, libraries, and applications. Regardless of the underlying physical hardware, this encapsulation ensures that the software operating within the virtual machine (VM) interacts with a constant environment. A Type 1 (bare metal) or Type 2 (hosted) hypervisor, which manages the virtual machines (VMs) and allots physical resources like CPU, memory, and storage, is in charge of the virtualization layer. As a result, virtual machines (VMs) provide an abstraction layer that permits the coexistence of several OS on a single physical computer, each running in its own private virtualized environment.

On the other hand, although the underlying technologies—Linux cgroups and namespaces, for example—have been around for a while, containers reflect a more recent paradigm. Dockers run at the OS level, unlike virtual machines (VMs), which virtualize at the hardware level. A program and all necessary libraries, binaries, and configuration files are bundled into a container, which shares the host system's kernel rather than a whole operating system stack. As a result, overhead is greatly reduced, enabling containers to be small, quick, and flexible. Applications operate consistently in various contexts, from a developer's desktop workstation to a production server, due to the isolation containers offer.

There are various implications for this basic architectural distinction between containers and virtual machines. Firstly, compared to virtual machines (VMs), which may take minutes to start up, containers can be started up in seconds, if not milliseconds, due to their lightweight design. Because of their pace, containers are an excellent fit for today's dynamic environments, where services and applications must grow quickly to meet demand. Moreover, a single server can host more containers than virtual machines (VMs) because containers don't carry the weight of full OS instances.

Still, the benefits of containers don't make virtual machines any less useful. Because virtual machines (VMs) run separate kernel instances, they offer a higher level of isolation. This isolation can be essential when using programs that need strict security restrictions or when many OS versions and types must run on the same physical server. Furthermore, as virtual machines have developed over time, a robust tool ecosystem, extensive documentation, and recognized best practices have resulted.

Each has its own management and orchestration ecosystem, whether for virtual machines or containers. Virtual machine solutions such as VMware vSphere and Microsoft Hyper-V provide all-inclusive management tools for deploying, tracking, and maintaining virtual machines. Conversely, containers have led to the emergence of platforms such as Docker and orchestration tools like Kubernetes, which meet their unique requirements by providing easier networking, scalability, and deployment.

Containers frequently result in more effective resource use from an operational and resource perspective. Containers use less system resources since they run on a single OS kernel and do not require the redundancy of operating numerous OS instances. This efficiency might result in cost savings, particularly in cloud contexts where resource utilization directly affects billing.

However, the issue between containers and virtual machines (VMs) must be approached without absolute power. Using containers in place of virtual machines (VMs) is not the issue. Rather, the key is to comprehend the advantages and disadvantages of every strategy and apply them where they are most effective. For example, a hybrid approach combining the agility and efficiency of containers with the strong isolation of virtual machines (VMs) is becoming increasingly common. In this approach, container orchestration platforms are run and isolated within virtual machines.

In conclusion, the discussion surrounding virtual machines and containers represents a broader shift in software development and deployment approaches. The methods and technologies we employ also evolve along with the needs of contemporary applications, which include increased expectations for efficiency, scalability, and adaptability. Due to the fundamental qualities of virtual machines and containers, they have carved out distinct niches in this environment. Although containers present a novel and efficient method for deploying applications, virtual machines (VMs) continue to be a reliable and well-proven option for several use cases. It is more productive to think of them as complementary tools in an ever-expanding toolset, each with a role to play in influencing the direction of software, as opposed to seeing them as competing technologies.

## Advantages of containerization

The field of technology is characterized by the continuous development of tools and approaches aimed at streamlining procedures and improving results, especially in software development and deployment. In the midst of this dynamic, containerization has become a powerful force, mostly because of the many benefits it provides. When we explore the intricacies of containerization, it becomes evident that this methodology not only expedites software development but also ushers in a new era of operational efficacy and adaptability.

Fundamentally, containerization is the process of encapsulating an application with all its dependencies inside a "container." This methodology guarantees that the application functions uniformly in various computing contexts. This technique was born out of the necessity for consistency, which is a constant source of difficulty for developers. How often have experts lamented that a piece of software "works on my machine" only to discover inconsistencies in other settings? The use of containers solves this problem effectively. Containers guarantee consistent application behavior regardless of the operating system and platform by encapsulating the application, libraries, binaries, and configuration files. This consistency can streamline the entire software deployment lifecycle by considerably lowering the friction typically encountered during the transition from development to production.

Beyond consistency's allure, containerization is notable for its efficiency. Conventional virtualization methods, like virtual machines (VMs), include a significant overhead because they bear the load of a whole operating system. In contrast, containers share the OS kernel of the host system, eliminating the requirement for individual OS instances for every application. Due to this design feature, containers are extremely quick and light. Because of their rapid instantiation and termination capabilities, they offer highly valued agility in contemporary software development situations, especially in pipelines for continuous integration and continuous deployment (CI/CD).

Another advantage of containerization is scalability. Modern applications must adapt to the rise and fall of user demand, particularly those hosted in cloud environments. Today's software must scale on the go, whether it's a retail application that experiences a spike during a sale or a financial tool that sees surges at the end of the month. Because containers are lightweight, they can be swiftly spun up or down, which makes it easy for applications to adjust to variations in demand. This dynamic scalability helps to ensure optimal performance, which improves user experience. It also helps to utilize resources, which may result in cost savings efficiently.

One of the main benefits of containerization is isolation, which offers several benefits. Every container functions independently, protecting its internal operations from outside disruptions. Because of this isolation, programs are guaranteed to operate in a safe, regulated environment free from interference from other applications. It also enables developers to operate on specific containerized microservices without interfering with other application components. This division encourages modular development, which allows various teams to work on different services concurrently, increasing output and teamwork.

The contribution of containerization to DevOps processes is another crucial benefit. By merging development and operations, DevOps seeks to close the gaps that have historically existed between these two fields and improve efficiency and collaboration. It is the nature of containers to support this paradigm. Application development, deployment, and scaling are just a few of the tasks that DevOps teams may automate with tools like Docker for container creation and Kubernetes for orchestration. These automations ensure that software is deployed in a stable, dependable manner by speeding up operations and lowering human error rates.

Moreover, containerization offers a greater degree of freedom in selecting and utilizing software stacks. Developers are freed from the limitations of system-wide software versions because every container is self-sufficient and comes with all the dependencies an application needs. Multiple containers, each with a different set of libraries and binaries, can operate simultaneously on a system without causing conflicts. Because of this flexibility, applications are not restricted by system-wide deployments and may be created with the best tools and technology.

Lastly, it is impossible to ignore how containerization promotes reproducibility and version control. Manifest files, such as Dockerfiles, are frequently used to build containers. These files include information about the program, its dependencies, and the runtime environment. Versioning these files enables teams to precisely reproduce setups, roll back to earlier configurations, and track changes. This kind of reproducibility is quite helpful, particularly when troubleshooting or trying to keep development, testing, and production environments uniform.

In conclusion, containerization is more than simply a fleeting trend in the huge field of software development. This revolutionary method tackles numerous issues that have traditionally been connected to software design, implementation, and expansion. There are numerous benefits associated with containerization, ranging from guaranteeing consistency and scalability to encouraging effective use of resources and supporting DevOps. Containerization is a bright spot of efficiency and flexibility for enterprises looking to be responsive, competitive, and agile in the current digital world. It has the potential to influence software development in the years to come significantly.

## The rise of Docker

Few technologies have made such a significant influence in such a short period of time in the history of software development and deployment as Docker. This platform has transformed application deployment methodologies and fundamentally changed how organizations approach software development. It was the driving force behind the modern era of containerization. In order to comprehend Docker's explosive growth, it is essential to examine its beginnings, key characteristics, and software-related problems it solved.

The history of Docker started in 2013, when dotCloud, a platform-as-a-service provider, was founded. The goal of the open-source Docker project, launched by dotCloud creator Solomon Hykes, is to build application containers that are small, lightweight, portable, and self-sufficient. In essence, Docker offered a technology to automatically launch applications inside lightweight containers, ensuring that the applications operated reliably in various computer systems. Although the idea of containers wasn't totally novel—technologies like Linux namespaces and cgroups had already established the foundation—Docker's groundbreaking approach to democratizing and streamlining containerization was.

A major factor in Docker's success has been its prompt solution to a recurring problem in software development: the consistency challenge. The notorious "it works on my machine" problem, in which software operated randomly while moving from development to production because of environmental variances, challenged developers for years. Docker's container-centric design addressed this problem directly. Docker guaranteed that applications had all they needed to operate reliably regardless of the underlying environment by combining them with the required binaries, libraries, and configuration files. Successfully bridging the gap between development and operations helped launch DevOps methods into a new era.

Another important factor in Docker's success was its easy use. With its user-friendly command-line interface and Dockerfile, a declarative file that outlined the procedures for creating a container, Docker abstracted the complexity of containerization. To utilize Docker's features, developers only needed to adhere to the simple instructions; they didn't need to be experts in container technology. Docker's adoption was accelerated by its simplicity, making it available to many developers and businesses.

Additionally, a major factor in Docker's success was its approach to image management, which was made possible by means of the Docker Hub. A collaborative environment was fostered by the ability of developers to exchange, reuse, and improve upon pre-existing container setups through the Docker Hub, a repository of container images. Because of this collective sharing, developers were able to utilize the community's collective expertise, which sped up development cycles and promoted best practices, rather than always having to start from zero.

When compared to conventional virtual machines, Docker's architecture—particularly its utilization of a single, shared operating system kernel—made it incredibly lightweight. Faster startup times and effective resource use were the results of this. These kinds of efficiency translated into real cost reductions in an era where resources were metered and billed, and organizations were moving to the cloud. Because of its cost-effectiveness and technical advantages, Docker has become a desirable option for both new and established businesses.

Another feature of Docker's architecture was extensibility and integration. As Docker containers spread, it became clear that orchestration—or managing the lifetime of containers—was necessary. Acknowledging this, the Docker community grew and gave rise to orchestration tools like Kubernetes, which automates deployment, scaling, and management, and Docker Compose, which defines multi-container applications. Docker's place in the software deployment ecosystem was further solidified by its ability to work seamlessly with these tools.

Another important factor in Docker's success was that it is an open-source project. DotCloud made sure that Docker benefited from the combined knowledge of a worldwide developer community by making it open-source. Rapid modifications, enhancements, and the creation of a robust ecosystem of plugins, extensions, and integrations were made possible by this community-driven approach.

Since companies and developers could review the code, participate in its development, and make sure it complied with industry standards, being open-source also increased trust.

Finally, Docker entered the market at a moment when it was ready for change. A platform like Docker was able to flourish because of the convergence of microservices design, the cloud computing revolution, and the push for DevOps methods. Docker was not only a convenient tool but also essential for modern software deployment strategies because it offered the tooling and methodology that perfectly matched these trends.

In conclusion, Docker's success is evidence of innovation's power when it addresses real-world problems in the industry. Docker made a name for itself in the software industry by providing a sophisticated, user-friendly, and effective answer to the age-old problem of program consistency. Its influence extends beyond containerization; it emphasizes the value of community cooperation, the possibilities of open-source, and the necessity of ongoing adaptation in response to market trends. Software development chapters will surely come to recognize Docker's impact as a turning point in the field as time goes on.

# CHAPTER II

# Setting Up Docker

## System requirements

Docker is a software development platform that has revolutionized the packaging, distribution, and execution of applications in various computing settings. Its adaptability and cross-platform capabilities have contributed to its rapid rise to the forefront of containerization technologies. But in order to fully utilize Docker, you have to make sure that the underlying system satisfies the necessary requirements. This section explores Docker's system requirements, explaining the requirements for various operating systems and the architectural factors that help ensure a seamless Docker experience.

Docker's system requirements are dependent on the host operating system because its fundamental architecture depends on its ability to utilize the kernel functionalities of the operating system. Let's analyze these specifications in light of widely used operating systems.

As Docker's original platform, Linux has long been a favorite among system administrators and developers. Cgroups and namespaces are two Linux kernel technologies that Docker directly uses to support containerization. Consequently, a suitable kernel version is the main prerequisite for Docker on Linux. Docker works well with the majority of contemporary Linux variants running kernel versions 3.10 or higher. Nonetheless, in order to take advantage of the newest features and security improvements, it is advised to utilize a more current kernel version.

Ubuntu, Debian, Fedora, and CentOS are the Linux distributions on which Docker has been thoroughly tested. Although Docker can be used with other distributions, these are still the most widely used and supported options. Furthermore, Docker requires a 64-bit platform in order to function properly and manage memory.

An important turning point was reached when Docker was integrated into the Windows ecosystem, demonstrating Docker's dedication to cross-platform operability. With Docker Desktop for Windows, you can run Docker containers natively on Windows by using either Hyper-V or Windows Subsystem for Linux 2 (WSL 2), depending on how you have it configured. Some prerequisites are crucial for a seamless Docker experience on Windows.

First off, a 64-bit version of Windows 10 Pro, Enterprise, or Education is required for Docker Desktop to function. Docker's compatibility with Windows 10 Home was enhanced with the release of WSL 2. Given their importance in virtualization, Hyper-V and SLAT (Second Level Address Translation) also need to be enabled. In addition, the system needs to have a BIOS-level configuration to guarantee that Hardware-Assisted Virtualization is enabled and supported. Finally, in order to take advantage of WSL 2-based containers, you must install a supported Linux distribution from the Windows Store and enable the WSL 2 features.

Docker Desktop for Mac, a native program that uses Apple's Hypervisor.framework for virtualization, is the result of Docker's entry into the macOS ecosystem. The requirements are really simple for users of macOS. Docker requires macOS El Capitan 10.11 or later, 64-bit operating system. The most recent macOS version should be used for best features and performance. A Mac with Intel hardware is also required because Docker Desktop uses virtualization. However, recent advancements can see modifications for the more recent Apple Silicon architecture.

Some general prerequisites and concerns apply to Docker's setup regardless of the platform, in addition to the operating system needs. Disk space, for example, is an important factor. Volumes, logs, containers, and images for Docker can build up and use a lot of storage. As a result, having enough disk space is essential. A minimum of 20GB is advised, however actual requirements can vary based on the applications and images involved.

Memory is essential to Docker's functionality as well. Although 2GB may be the absolute minimum, at least 4GB is advised for any realistic, real-world use. Even more memory allocation is necessary for more demanding workloads, such managing several containers or using memory-intensive applications.

Another essential component of Docker's setup is network configuration. An unhindered network connection is necessary because Docker containers frequently need to communicate with outside services. Additionally, a steady and quick internet connection can greatly speed up the setup and deployment process because Docker images are fetched from Docker Hub or other registries.

Finally, a system that makes updating updates simple is required by Docker's regular and dynamic update cycle. Updating Docker guarantees access to important security updates as well as the newest features. Using an out-of-date version of Docker can put systems at undue risk, especially considering the constantly changing landscape of cybersecurity threats.

In conclusion, Docker has certain system requirements even if its claim to be able to "Build, Ship, and Run Any App, Anywhere" highlights its versatility. The ability to fully utilize Docker depends on having a solid awareness of these requirements, ranging from the unique demands of various operating systems to the standard requirements of disk space, memory, and network. These specifications may change as Docker develops and fits into newer systems and technologies. However, their core will continue to focus on ensuring Docker is seamless, efficient, and secure.

## Installing Docker on Windows, Mac, and Linux

Docker is a brilliant example of effective software deployment in today's digital world, providing a uniform environment across a variety of platforms. Docker, which promises containerized applications, has grown to be a vital tool for system administrators, developers, and businesses. However, navigating the installation process is a requirement for starting the containerization journey.

This section aims to guide readers through the subtleties of installing Docker on three popular operating systems: Linux, Mac, and Windows.

With Docker's inclusion, Windows—which has never been the first choice for developers inclined toward containerization—saw a radical change. The main tool for this is Docker Desktop for Windows, which provides a native Windows program that lets users take advantage of Docker containers' capabilities without having to dual-boot or use virtual machines.

Before starting the installation, users must confirm that their system meets Docker's requirements. In particular, 64-bit versions of Windows 10 Pro, Enterprise, or Education are required. It's also necessary to enable Hyper-V, Hardware-Assisted Virtualization, and Second Level Address Translation (SLAT). Enabling WSL 2 and having a supported Linux distribution installed from the Windows Store are essential for anyone eager to use Windows Subsystem for Linux 2 (WSL 2) for a more Linux-centric experience.

The installation process is simple in and of itself. The Docker Desktop installer can be launched by downloading it from Docker's official website. The installer usually consists of a sequence of prompts. After installation, the Docker Desktop program can be accessed from the system tray and provides an easy-to-use interface for managing images, settings, and Docker containers.

Docker, for macOS enthusiasts, hasn't been a distant dream. Because Docker Desktop for Mac was designed with the macOS ecosystem in mind, it operates using Apple's Hypervisor.framework, eliminating the need for extra virtualization software and guaranteeing a seamless experience.

The minimal system requirements for macOS are as follows. Docker requires a 64-bit version of macOS El Capitan 10.11 or later. Initially, Docker required Intel hardware in order to virtualize, but there is increasing expectation that Apple Silicon will be supported in later versions.

To obtain the Docker Desktop for Mac installer and install Docker on macOS, go to the official Docker website. Installing Docker.app is as simple as dragging it into the Applications folder after it has been downloaded. Docker.app may ask for rights when it launches for the first time in order to install its networking components and other requirements. Permissions like this must be granted in order for Docker to function properly. After this, Docker resides in the menu bar, giving users easy access to all of its features, just like its Windows equivalent.

For Docker enthusiasts, Linux, the platform upon which Docker originated, delivers the most natural and integrated experience. It should come as no surprise that Docker's installation on Linux is both simple and flexible, considering its extensive origins in Linux kernel capabilities.

But the world of Linux, with its multitude of distributions, necessitates a somewhat fragmented approach. Although Docker supports a wide range of distributions, we'll concentrate on the most popular ones—Ubuntu, Debian, Fedora, and CentOS—in order to keep things concise.

The process starts for Ubuntu users with updating the apt package index. Installing required programs such as apt-transport-https, ca-certificates, curl, software-properties-common, and gnupg-agent is possible with updated repositories. After this, users can make sure that Docker is being downloaded from reliable sources by adding the official GPG key for Docker and configuring the stable repository. Installing Docker Engine is the last step, and it can be done with a simple apt command.

CentOS, Fedora, and Debian users would find the procedure similar, though with a few slight adjustments. Fedora enthusiasts would interact with dnf commands, while Debian users would use apt commands to mimic the Ubuntu approach. In contrast, CentOS depends on the yum package manager.

Not to mention, Docker comes in two versions: Docker EE (Enterprise Edition) and Docker CE (Community Edition). Docker CE is sufficient for most individual users and developers, whereas Docker EE's enterprise capabilities make it suitable for larger businesses and organizations.

Regardless of the distribution, it is recommended that the user be added to the Docker group after installation in order to guarantee that Docker commands can be run without root privileges. Furthermore, you may guarantee that Docker will always be available on your machine by setting it to launch automatically at boot and starting the Docker service.

In conclusion, the Docker installation process is still based on ease of use and simplicity even though it varies depending on the platform. Whether it's the command-line sophistication of Linux distributions or the graphical power of Docker Desktop for Windows and Mac, Docker ensures that users, irrespective of their platform allegiance, get a seamless introduction to the world of containerization. Installation procedures may change as Docker develops further and fits into newer architectures and systems. However, the fundamental idea—making Docker efficient, secure, and available to all—will always stand.

## Basic Docker commands and verification

Within the software development community, Docker has become a symbol of effective application deployment, promoting consistency and dependability in a variety of settings. Developers and system administrators need to grasp Docker's basic commands as they enter the world of containerized development. These commands provide information about the state and health of containers in addition to controlling Docker interactions. By explaining the fundamental Docker commands and exploring their verification, this section ensures that users can fully utilize Docker's capabilities.

Docker's architecture is command-line structured, based on images and containers. Images represent applications' blueprints, and the instances that run once they are generated are known as containers. Understanding the commands that control these objects and the overall Docker system is necessary to interact with Docker efficiently.

Managing and deploying images is a fundamental aspect of Docker's capabilities. The basic parts of a container are called Docker images, which can be obtained through resources like Docker Hub.

The most fundamental command for anyone looking to retrieve an image from a repository is docker pull. Downloading the desired image to one's local machine requires users to provide the image's name, potentially followed by a version tag. Once obtained, docker images, also known as docker image ls, provide a comprehensive overview of the local repository by allowing users to display all images that are available on their system.

Another key component of Docker's usefulness is the ability to create customized images that are suited to particular applications. This is made possible when the docker build command is used and pointed to a directory containing a Dockerfile. A custom image is created by Docker using instructions from the Dockerfile. When the build command is executed, Docker uses these directives to create the image.

After images are used as the foundation, generating containers makes sense. This is done through the probably most flexible command in Docker's toolkit, the docker run command. This command can map ports, set environment variables, instantiate containers in detached or foreground modes, and more depending on the flags and parameters provided. In essence, a docker run converts an image from a static blueprint into a functioning program.

Managing and keeping an eye on these live containers is also essential. When the docker ps command is used, a list of all the currently operating containers is displayed, together with information about each one such as its ID, name, port, and base image. To get a longer list that includes both stopped and operating containers, use docker ps -a.

Throughout the container management lifecycle, stopping, pausing, and restarting containers are frequent activities. These demands are met by commands like docker stop, docker start, docker restart, and docker pause, giving users control over their containers' lifetime and status.

Occasionally, it becomes necessary to go at a container's logs or run commands inside of it. Users may examine the log output of an active container with the docker logs command, which is very helpful for monitoring and debugging. With docker exec, users may run commands inside a running container for a more interactive experience. This can be used in conjunction with a shell such as bash for a full-featured terminal experience.

Remaining images, containers, and volumes may build up when users interact with Docker over time, creating clutter and even putting resource limits on users. A set of commands Docker provides can be used to manage and clean up these entities. Users can uninstall images and containers using the docker rm and docker rmi commands, respectively. Docker system prune, which gets rid of all stopped containers, unused networks, and hanging images, can be used for a more thorough cleanup.

It is crucial to confirm Docker's configuration and functionality in addition to managing entities. To make sure users are aware of the version of Docker they have installed, the docker --version or docker version command offers information about the version of Docker. Docker info is the go-to command for delving further into Docker's setup and system information. It provides information on the Docker client, server, images, containers, and the underlying system.

Networking is another essential component of the Docker ecosystem. Knowing Docker's networking is crucial since containers frequently need to communicate with one another and the outside world. While docker network inspect gives you comprehensive details about a particular network, docker network ls gives you an overview of all the available networks.

In conclusion, the uninitiated may find Docker intimidating due to its complex architecture and wide range of features. On the other hand, users can become excellent Docker practitioners by mastering the basic commands. Docker interactions revolve around these commands, which can be used for managing images, controlling containers, or ensuring Docker is operating properly. While these commands may be expanded or refined as Docker continues its evolutionary path, their fundamental nature will not change, enabling smooth, effective, and transparent interactions with Docker's containerized world.

# CHAPTER III

## Docker Architecture

### Overview of Docker components

Docker is a paradigm shift in modern software development and deployment that is changing how applications are developed, deployed, and used. However, beneath Docker's intuitive commands and seamless functioning are a multitude of components, each essential to Docker's current state of power. This section aims to provide a comprehensive grasp of the complex machinery that powers Docker by dissecting these components.

Docker Engine is a server-side application that is at the core of Docker's functionality; it builds and runs Docker containers. The engine, consisting of a server, a REST API, and a command-line interface (CLI), supports every major task Docker performs. Operating as a daemon process, the server performs the bulk of the work, with CLI interacting with the server through commands. By serving as a conduit, the REST API allows software programs to interact with the daemon, extending Docker's functionality outside of the CLI.

Images and containers are the basic components that make up Docker. The application, dependencies, libraries, and other binaries required for an application to run are all contained in an image, which is similar to a static snapshot. An image can be compared to a blueprint, the unchangeable base from which containers are created. Conversely, containers are live instances of these images that are dynamic in nature. They provide platform consistency by encapsulating the application in a runtime environment. Docker's concept is based on this contrast between images and containers, where images are the static genesis and containers are the dynamic offspring.

The Dockerfile is a small but powerful file that controls the creation of Docker images. A Dockerfile is similar to a script; it consists of a sequence of instructions, each of which does a particular job, such as installing applications or establishing the base image. The engine reads these directives when the docker build command is used with a Dockerfile, producing a Docker image in accordance with the guidelines. A vital component of the Docker ecosystem, Dockerfiles allow you to design and automate the production of images.

Although individual containers can be easily managed using Docker's native commands, real-world applications typically require a collection of connected containers, each with a distinct function. This need is met by Docker Compose, a tool for creating and managing multi-container Docker applications. Users can create a cohesive tapestry of containers by defining volumes, networks, and services in a docker-compose.yml file. This entire ensemble can be instantiated with a single docker-compose up command, which is why Docker Compose is a great tool for both system administrators and developers.

A system for storing, sharing, and distributing Docker images becomes essential as developers continue to develop and improve them. This function is performed by the cloud-based registry service Docker Hub. It enables developers to publish their personalized images to the cloud, granting others access. Additionally, Docker Hub is a repository from which users can obtain images of widely used software applications and services. It is filled with official and community-driven images. Private registries exist outside of Docker Hub, allowing businesses to keep their proprietary images safe and secure.

Modern applications are built on connectivity. Networking is essential for container communication and other interfaces with external services. Docker's built-in networking features make sure containers can communicate effectively. Several network modes, including overlay, none, bridge, and host, are available by default with Docker. Each mode is tailored to a particular use case, from straightforward isolated networks to more intricate multi-host networking for swarm services. With the option to establish custom networks as well, Docker guarantees that developers will have the flexibility and granularity necessary to design the network architecture for their applications.

For many applications, data storage and persistence are essential. Despite the transient nature of containers, Docker Volumes guarantee that data survives in the event that the container fails. Data can be persistently saved outside of the container's file system by means of volumes, which are specified and controlled by Docker. Docker Volumes provide a way to store data, logs, configuration files, and database data, so that it may be accessed by containers running now and in the future. Decoupling data from the container's lifespan improves reliability and flexibility.

Docker Swarm develops as Docker's native clustering and orchestration solution in an era where scalability and high availability are not just desirable, but frequently necessary. With Swarm, users can generate and manage a swarm—a group of machines running Docker, called nodes. Services, which are tasks carried out on nodes, ensure that the application remains in the appropriate condition. Docker Swarm provides a range of features that meet these objectives, including rolling updates, fault tolerance, and expanding the quantity of container instances.

In conclusion, Docker appears to have a straightforward and user-friendly interface, but its functionality is supported by several components, each essential to its operation. Every element of Docker, from the essential Docker Engine to the sophisticated orchestration capabilities of Docker Swarm, contributes to its status as the top containerization technology. Users will find it increasingly important to comprehend these elements and how they interact as they learn more about Docker. This information not only helps users better utilize Docker's features but also provides insight into the innovative architecture and design that Docker represents.

## How Docker works

Docker has become a revolutionary tool in the complex world of software development, revolutionizing program creation, deployment, and scaling. Essentially, Docker offers a containerization framework, enabling programmers to package software into standardized settings, referred to as containers. However, what does this actually mean, and how does Docker pull this off? We need to investigate Docker's architecture, components, and fundamental ideas in order to comprehend its complex inner workings.

Docker's unique architecture is the foundation of its functionality. Docker concentrates on the application and its dependencies as opposed to traditional virtualization, which is based on simulating full machines, also called Virtual Machines or VMs. This implies that Docker virtualizes the operating system itself rather than the hardware and numerous instances of the operating system. Applications running in Docker containers share the same OS kernel but function in separate user areas, resulting in a lightweight and efficient system.

The Docker Engine, a client-server program consisting of three main components—a server, a REST API, and a command-line interface (CLI)—is the essential element that makes this architecture possible. The daemon process runs the server and is initiated by issuing the dockerd command. Programs can utilize the interfaces specified by the REST API to communicate with the daemon and give it instructions. In contrast, the CLI is a command-line utility that uses scriptable commands to interact with the daemon. The daemon carries out the work after receiving a command from the user, such as docker run, which is transmitted to it by the CLI.

Images and containers are key concepts in Docker's functionality. A Docker image is a small, executable, standalone software package that contains all the components required to run an application, such as the runtime, system libraries, application code, system tools, and settings. Images are unchangeable, or immutable. Docker builds a container from an image when developers wish to launch it. An executable instance of an image is called a container. The container is the actual execution environment that contains the running application, whereas the image specifies the application and its requirements.

The Dockerfile is another essential part of the Docker ecosystem. Developers use this script to define and explain an image's layers. Layer by layer, Docker images are constructed. A Dockerfile's instructions each generate a new layer in the image. The method is more efficient when modifications are made to an image since only the modified layers are updated and not the entire application.

Additionally, Docker offers a centralized infrastructure for sharing and distributing container images, known as Docker Hub. By pushing their customized images to Docker Hub, developers can make them publicly accessible. Alternatively, users can use Docker Hub's publicly accessible images for their projects. A vast library of ready-to-use images for a variety of uses, including base OS images like Ubuntu and Alpine and application-specific images like

WordPress or MongoDB, has been accumulated as a result of this collaborative ecosystem.

Another aspect of Docker's complex inner workings is its network management. Containers can be allocated to specific networks when they are running. By default, Docker offers three types of networks: host, none, and bridge. Every one has a distinct function. For example, the host network offers direct, non-isolated access to the host's network, whereas the bridge network enables communication across containers under the same bridge. In order to guarantee that containers have the necessary connectivity, isolation, and network circumstances, Docker also enables users to define custom networks.

Managing and storing data in Docker requires volume management. In contrast to containers' transient nature, which results in data loss upon destruction, volumes possess persistence and independence. This implies that data is persistent and can be retrieved by subsequent containers. Volumes offer a method to backup, restore, or transfer data without being connected to the lifecycle of a container. They can also be shared and utilized across containers.

In conclusion, Docker works by balancing a number of various components and concepts. Docker seamlessly integrates complex processes to deliver a containerization experience, from its unique OS-level virtualization to its effective image and container management. Operating at the core of this system is the Docker Engine, which processes and executes user commands through its daemon, API, and CLI. The fundamental components of application deployment are images and containers, but networks, volumes,

Dockerfiles, and Docker Hub enhance the containerization process by offering adaptability, cooperation, and durability. All things considered, Docker provides a confined, reliable, and effective software development and deployment environment, solidifying its status as an essential tool in today's technological landscape.

# CHAPTER IV

# Working with Docker Images

## Understanding Docker images

Docker has made a name for itself in the containerization space by revolutionizing software deployment and orchestration methods. Although the dynamic nature of Docker containers is frequently highlighted, the foundation of this transformation lies with the Docker images. Examining Docker images reveals their fundamental structure, essence, and significance inside the Docker ecosystem.

Docker images serve as static, unchangeable blueprints that give rise to vibrant, dynamic containers. If one were to compare a Docker image to a class in the context of programming, the container would be the instance of that class. An image is a comprehensive representation of all the components an application needs to function. It contains the runtime, system tools, environment configurations, application code, and necessary libraries. By combining these components, Docker images guarantee that a container has everything it needs to run smoothly when it is instantiated, regardless of the host environment.

The difficulties that Docker images attempt to solve reveal their power. The difference between development and production environments was a common problem in traditional software deployment. Even though a software item runs perfectly on a developer's workstation, it may not run smoothly on a production server. Variations in system libraries, settings, or other program requirements caused these discrepancies. Docker images became a remedy for this problem because of their thorough encapsulation. They provide consistent behavior across all deployment settings by bundling the program and its whole operational surroundings.

Examining the architecture of Docker images exposes a complex system that has been meticulously constructed. An image is made up of a stack of discrete layers, each of which represents a different adjustment or set of guidelines. Once a layer is formed, it cannot be altered. Because of its immutability, deployments are consistent and there is less chance of unintended changes. The fact that these layers can be shared by multiple images also promotes optimization. For example, Docker effectively reuses the underlying OS layer when building several images instead of duplicating it, which improves performance and conserves disk space.

A Dockerfile is used to manage the creation of a Docker image. This text document outlines a series of instructions that Docker follows while creating an image. A layer in the final image corresponds to each directive. Docker reads the Dockerfile and runs the directives one after the other by using the docker build command. The result is a layered image that is built according to the Dockerfile's specifications. By establishing a consistent, repeatable process for creating images, this approach removes uncertainty and guarantees that images can be precisely replicated even when developed by different teams or on various systems.

After being created, these Docker images frequently need to be shared with colleagues, deployed across several servers, or made available to the whole public. Docker repositories like Docker Hub protect these images. Developers are able to add their images to these repositories and categorize them differently for each version. On the other hand, they can extract images, whether they are official images for widely used software tools, custom images, or versions developed by the community. Version control, distribution, and accessibility of Docker images are made simple by this ecosystem.

Nevertheless, Docker images' greatness extends beyond their masterful architecture. Their essence has championed the idea of "Build Once, Run Anywhere," ushering in a transformational approach on software deployment. This motto wasn't very clear in the days before containers. It becomes a physical reality with Docker images. Docker images help ensure that software acts consistently whether it is running on a development laptop, a testing server, or a cloud-based production environment by encapsulating all dependencies, from system libraries to environment variables.

Moreover, Docker images differ from conventional virtualization paradigms due to their lightweight design. In contrast to virtual machines, which contain the full guest operating system, Docker images just contain the application and its immediate dependencies. Smaller image sizes from this simplified method led to quicker deployments, more effective scaling, and more cost-effective resource use.

In conclusion, the unsung heroes of the containerization story are Docker images. They offer the fundamental integrity that is necessary for the vibrant world of Docker containers to flourish. Their carefully constructed architecture, which includes immutability and layered design, guarantees portability, efficiency, and consistency. Repositories such as Docker Hub ensure distribution and accessibility, while the Dockerfile-driven creation process ensures repetition and accuracy. Docker images bridge the gap between development and production environments by encapsulating the idea of seamless, consistent software deployments. Understanding Docker images thoroughly is essential as containerization continues to shape software delivery in the future. They are essentially the cornerstone of Docker's software development and deployment revolution.

## Building images using Dockerfiles

Docker's containerization paradigm is brilliant not only because it allows for lightweight, isolated containers but also because it provides reliable, repeatable techniques for building these containers. The Dockerfile, a straightforward yet effective tool that enables developers to specify and automate the image building process, is essential to this reproducibility. The Dockerfile acts as a guide for Docker, outlining the actions, settings, and parts needed to build an image. This section explores the world of Dockerfiles, including its structure, importance, and crucial role in the development of Docker.

In essence, Dockerfiles are plaintext scripts made up of a series of directives that specify different steps or setups related to the image building process. Their methodical strategy involves laying down a foundational base and then adding layers one after the other, much like a mason building a wall brick by brick. This methodical methodology guarantees the transparent and repeatable creation of Docker images. Unpredictable differences will no longer plague software deployment because the final image will always be the same if the Dockerfile is left unaltered, regardless of where or when an image is generated.

The fundamental layer, which is typically indicated by the FROM directive, is the core of any Dockerfile. This layer usually refers to a base image that is superimposed by subsequent layers, such as an operating system or runtime environment. The Dockerfile builds upon this basis by articulating several levels, each corresponding to a distinct directive. This may be using the COPY directive to copy application code into the image, the RUN command to install any required software, the ENV directive to configure environment variables, or the CMD or ENTRYPOINT directives to define the default executable for the container.

Caching layers while the image is being built is one of the key characteristics of Dockerfile. Docker caches the layers created by each directive in a Dockerfile for efficiency. This implies that Docker simply reconstructs the layers from the point of change, reusing the cached layers for previous steps, if a developer makes changes to a Dockerfile and rebuilds the image. During the image development process, this caching approach significantly speeds up the image construction process, especially when iterating on an image. It's important to remember that cache consumption necessitates cautious Dockerfile design. To maximize the benefits of caching, frequently updated instructions should be positioned towards the end of the Dockerfile.

However, Dockerfiles are not merely a series of commands. They are the embodiment of best practices and norms that improve the final images' efficiency, security, and size. For example, although using a fully functional OS as a base image may be tempting, best practices recommend using minimalist base images, such as Alpine Linux, which remove unnecessary components and reduce the image's footprint. Comparably, reducing the number of layers and, thus, the size of the image can be achieved by chaining several commands within a single RUN directive and separating them with conjunctions.

The immutability principle, which is essential to containerized deployments, is also upheld by Dockerfiles. An image is unchangeable once it is created. A new image is created and the Dockerfile is updated if the application or any of its dependencies need to be updated. Because each image represents a snapshot of the application and its environment at a particular moment in time, this guarantees that deployments stay consistent. Furthermore, several image variations can coexist through version marking, allowing for incremental updates, rollbacks, or the simultaneous deployment of various versions.

Even while Dockerfiles have played a significant role in forming the Docker ecosystem, they still have some difficulties. It takes a deep understanding of Docker's complexities and the application that must be containerized to create an effective, secure Dockerfile. Vulnerabilities can be introduced by utilizing out-of-date base images, unintentionally incorporating sensitive data, or executing containers with elevated access. The community has developed best practices and tools to audit and improve Dockerfiles and ensure they adhere to the strict specifications of modern software deployments.

In conclusion, Dockerfiles are the meticulous creators of Docker images, carefully specifying their composition, functionality, and appearance. With their layered, sequential approach, they guarantee transparent, repeatable, and quick image generation. Their commitment to immutability ensures consistent deployments, and their built-in support for caching speeds up development iterations. Additionally, Dockerfiles maintain best practices by including protocols that improve image size, security, and efficiency. Dockerfiles hold a vital role in the ongoing transformation of the software deployment landscape, supporting the reproducibility and reliability that Docker offers. Understanding the art and science of Dockerfiles becomes not only helpful but essential for developers and businesses eager to take full advantage of Docker's capabilities. They are creating more than just Docker images when they write, build, and iterate using Dockerfiles; they are creating the framework that will allow their containerized applications to flourish.

## Pushing and pulling images from Docker Hub

In the dynamic world of Docker's containerization, using Dockerfiles to create Docker images is just half the story. Distributing and granting access to these images is the other essential component, which allows them to be implemented in a variety of settings, including large cloud infrastructures and local development workstations. Docker Hub, the official public registry for Docker images by default, is the perfect example of this distribution strategy. Developers can 'submit' customized images to the registry and 'pull' desired images to their local computers using Docker Hub, which functions as a repository for Docker images, much like a library holding a sizable collection of books. The intricacies and significance of pushing and pulling images from Docker Hub are explored in this section.

Docker Hub is the central nervous system of the Docker ecosystem, serving as more than just a storage solution. It functions as a centralized marketplace where open-source projects, big businesses, and individual developers may all publish and distribute their containerized applications to the wider public. The deployment process is greatly streamlined by the availability of popular software tools, databases, and services as Docker images, due to the simplicity with which images can be pushed to or pulled from Docker Hub, creating a thriving ecosystem.

Once an image is created, it may be pushed to Docker Hub. A Docker image created by a developer on their local computer usually lives solely in that developer's local Docker daemon. This image needs to be up on a central registry in order to be distributed across different environments or shared with others. The image is given a name before it is pushed, usually in the username/repository:tag format. This naming scheme guarantees Docker Hub storage that is hierarchical and well-organized. The repository indicates the image name, the tag enables versioning, and the username is linked to the Docker Hub account. Once the image has been appropriately tagged, the layers are sent to Docker Hub using the docker push command. It's important to note that only the differential layers are transmitted, guaranteeing a quick upload, assuming some layers of the image are already on Docker Hub from earlier pushes.

Conversely, pulling an image from Docker Hub is a similarly simple process. Docker Hub is frequently the first place a developer goes whether they want to launch a well-known database, test out a new programming language runtime, or retrieve a colleague's freshly released application. The desired image's name and optional tag are used to retrieve and save the image layers on the local Docker daemon. This is done by running the docker pull command. These images can be fetched and then instantiated as containers, prepared to fulfill their intended function. In addition to the explicit docker pull command, Docker's user-friendliness is demonstrated by the fact that even a basic docker run command using an image that is not locally installed will implicitly start a pull request.

However, the brilliant idea of Docker Hub goes beyond its push and pull operation. It provides several features that improve the experience of distributing images. Integrated build systems provide automated image builds straight from source code repositories, guaranteeing that Docker images with the most recent code changes are easily accessible. Setting up webhooks to alert or start other services after an image push is successful is possible. Features promoting collaboration make sharing and managing images easier for groups. Furthermore, Docker Hub is more than simply a public image store; it also facilitates private repositories, guaranteeing that sensitive or proprietary images are kept out of the hands of unauthorized users.

Although Docker Hub is the most popular public registry by default, pushing and pulling images also works with other registries. Businesses frequently use private Docker registries, either in-house or through cloud providers. These private registries guarantee security, compliance, and performance by giving enterprises more precise control over their images. However, the basic functions continue to be the same. The same well-known Docker commands are still used to push or pull images to and from these registries, but the repository names and authentication credentials have changed.

Upon consideration, the core of Docker's vision—to democratize and simplify software deployment—is embodied by Docker Hub and the related push and pull image protocols. Docker Hub has transformed software acquisition and deployment by providing a central repository filled with an abundance of easily accessible software tools and services. Developers can publish their works on a platform by pushing them, and pulling ensures that the general public can easily use these services.

In conclusion, pushing to and pulling from Docker Hub are essential components of the Docker system. They make sure that once Docker images are generated, they are actively shared, encouraging cooperation, creativity, and simplicity of use. With its push and pull dynamics, Docker Hub remains steadfast as the pivot, propelling the movement of containerized applications throughout the digital landscape as Docker's rise continues in the IT industry.

## Managing and organizing images

Docker's rapid ascent in the software industry is largely due to its claim to make application deployment simpler. Docker images, which are static snapshots that contain an application and its environment and are ready to be instantiated on several platforms, are essential to fulfilling this promise. But as more and more developers and organizations use Docker, they inevitably accumulate a large number of images, thus managing and organizing them becomes crucial. Well-chosen images can improve security, expedite deployment processes, and increase developer productivity. This section delves into the intricacies of managing and organizing Docker images, making sure these foundational assets remain structured, updated, and accessible.

The foundation of image management is the Docker command-line interface (CLI), a flexible tool that makes a wide range of tasks possible, from using docker images to show available images to using docker rmi to remove unwanted ones. Despite their simplicity, these commands are the first line of defense for managing images, allowing developers to swiftly evaluate, edit, or remove images from their local collections.

An essential component of Docker image organization is tagging. Every image can have one or more tags, essentially descriptors that frequently provide version numbers or particular setups. A carefully labeled image library can have a profound impact. For example, an image may have tags such as newest, v2.0, or v1.0, all of which refer to distinct versions of the same program. In addition to helping with version control, proper tagging guarantees that deployments remain reliable and consistent. Teams can always access the most recent, stable version of an application by routinely checking and updating these tags—especially the most recent one.

The possibility of accumulating outdated or unneeded images increases with the volume of images. If neglected, these dormant images might present possible security flaws and take up a lot of storage space. Regular reduction of these images is necessary. To help with this, tools such as docker image prune can automatically remove images that aren't related to any containers currently in use. Furthermore, it is essential to comprehend the dependency tree when eliminating images. Layers are the foundation of every Docker image, and several images may share these layers. It's important to be cautious so that removing a single image doesn't unintentionally remove another.

The routine update of base images is another essential component of efficient image management. A lot of Docker images are built on top of base images, which might be Debian or Alpine, two simple operating systems. Like any software, these base images are updated regularly to fix bugs and enhance functionality. Applications can be made to be both secure and performant by routinely pulling the most recent versions of these base images and then rebuilding dependent images.

One aspect of image management that is sometimes disregarded is storage optimization. Large Docker images can occasionally occur, particularly when they contain extensive applications with plenty of dependencies. Effectively crafted Dockerfiles, which specify the image generation procedure, might be crucial in reducing image sizes. Methods like multi-stage builds, in which the application is compiled on one image and run on a lighter one, can significantly reduce the final image size. Storage can be further optimized by proactively searching for and eliminating unnecessary files, combining several RUN instructions, and making use of .dockerignore files.

Still, managing Docker images isn't a task limited to a developer's desktop. Images are being kept and maintained in centralized repositories or registries like Docker Hub more often due to the popularity of cloud-native systems and container orchestration technologies like Kubernetes. Further considerations are necessary for effective management in these kinds of situations. To guarantee that picture collections stay organized and current, image naming conventions, public and private repository classification, and automated build and update pipelines can be implemented. Images can also be protected from any dangers by conducting routine audits of these repositories, putting up vulnerability scanning, and implementing access controls.

Creating a lifecycle management strategy for Docker images in scenarios involving numerous teams or large-scale deployments is critical. This means outlining distinct phases of an image's life, starting from inception and development and ending with deployment, rollback, and retirement. In addition to providing structure to the development and deployment processes, lifecycle management helps maintain compliance by guaranteeing that only verified and approved images move forward through the pipeline.

In conclusion, Docker's images represent both a strength and a possible weakness as it continues to reshape software deployment paradigms. Even though they are incredibly consistent and portable, they can become burdensome and disorganized if not handled properly. Hence, efficient Docker image management and organization are necessities rather than luxuries. Docker images can be effortlessly integrated into deployment pipelines by means of systematic tagging, periodic pruning, regular updates, storage optimization, and structured lifecycle management. By doing this, businesses and developers can fully utilize Docker's capabilities and ensure their applications are always secure, flexible, and prepared for deployment in the ever-changing digital environment.

# CHAPTER V

## Running Containers

**Creating, starting, and stopping containers**

The containerization revolution began with Docker, which has completely changed how software developers design, pack, and deploy applications. The main features of Docker are its isolated environments, lightweight containers, and application execution capabilities. Although images offer a static blueprint, applications are made operational through containers, which give these blueprints life. Containers have a lifespan that includes creation, initiation, and termination, just like any other dynamic entity. Understanding this lifecycle is essential to realizing Docker's greatest potential. This section sets out on an investigation to explore the subtleties involved in creating, starting, and stopping Docker containers.

When a Docker container is created, that is its origin. This phase is a little more complicated than it might seem, even while it could be easy to see it as just translating an image into a running instance. The basic process of creating a container involves setting up an environment, allocating resources, and configuring settings for the application that will eventually be executed. During this stage, the command docker create is essential. When used in conjunction with an image name (and possibly a tag), this command creates a container but doesn't launch it. This is a crucial distinction. The application within isn't now executing; rather, a favorable environment is awaiting its activation. It is reasonable to question the purpose of such a dormant state. Before the program launches, it provides developers with a window to further customize the container, including mounting volumes, changing network settings, and defining environment variables.

But once the container starts up, that's when the real magic happens. Encapsulated within the image, the static application suddenly becomes dynamic, prepared to process data, serve requests, and communicate with other services. The container is brought to life with the command docker start. Following this directive, the application running inside the container starts to run, using the resources allotted to it while functioning in a separate environment. Isolation is essential. Even though they are hosted on the same host, each container operates independently of the others. This guarantees consistency and stability by ensuring that outside changes do not impact applications. Starting a container involves more than just turning it on; it also involves making sure that the application inside runs in a predictable, optimal environment.

However, there comes a point when a container needs to be stopped just like any other process. This may be necessary for several reasons—a task that has been finished, an update that is needed, or a system reboot. A container can be gracefully ended with the command docker stop. It requests that the application stop running and exit by sending a SIGTERM signal. A SIGKILL signal will forcibly terminate an application if it does not comply within a certain amount of time. This is a purposefully phased strategy. Data integrity and possible corruption are avoided when an application terminates gracefully, allowing it to release resources, store its state, and finish any active transactions.

One could wonder if these states are everlasting. Does stopping a container cause it to explode? No, not quite. Stopped containers hang around, holding onto their internal states and settings. Applications can be resumed due to their persistence, allowing them to carry on with their work. This feature is encapsulated in the command docker restart, which permits containers to be stopped and then restarted to maintain continuity.

However, a container's lifecycle isn't limited to these distinct stages. With its extensive command set, Docker provides a wide range of container management activities. For example, docker run can be used to start and create a container in one step rather than two. It streamlines the procedure by combining the functions of docker start and docker create. Similar to this, the --rm flag with docker run guarantees that, after the container's execution, it is automatically removed, optimizing resource use, for containers that need to finish a task and then exit.

Container monitoring is yet another essential component of container management. Developers can diagnose problems or evaluate performance with the help of commands like docker logs, which reveal details about the actions of a container. In contrast, docker stats provides an instantaneous perspective of a container's resource usage, guaranteeing that applications continue to function smoothly and consume minimal resources. Moreover, containers are not unchangeable. You can temporarily pause containers without halting them by using commands like docker pause; to resume containers, use docker unpause. These features guarantee that containers continue to be flexible, meeting a range of operational needs.

Upon reflection, Docker's universe's atomic units, containers, represent a dynamic lifespan. Rather than being merely operational procedures, their creation, initiation, and termination are essential to Docker's ability to deliver reliable, isolated, and efficient software deployment. Every stage—whether it's the quiet pre-production stage after creation, the busy activity after launch, or the elegant wrap-up after termination—has a specific function that guarantees programs function as best they can.

In conclusion, knowledge of the nuances of container lifecycles becomes essential as the software landscape shifts more and more toward containerization. Developers may fully utilize Docker's capabilities by learning how to create, start, and stop containers. This will help to ensure that applications not only launch without a hitch but also flourish in the dynamic, demanding, and constantly changing digital environment.

## Mapping ports and volumes

Not only can Docker's containerization paradigm package applications in isolated contexts, but it can also seamlessly connect these environments with the host system, which is what makes it so appealing. Applications benefit from isolation but aren't islands unto themselves due to this integration, which is mostly accomplished through port and volume mapping. They are dynamic and interactive because they can communicate through networks, persist data, and interact with other systems. This section explores the basic ideas behind port and volume mapping in Docker, explaining its importance and workings within the larger framework of deploying containerized applications.

Any application or service's communication capabilities are at its core. This kind of communication frequently takes place through designated network ports in the digital sphere. A specific port is used by an application running inside a Docker container to communicate with users or other external entities. But neither the host system nor the wider network can directly access this internal port within the container. Here's where port mapping comes into play. A port on the host system is mapped to a port inside the container by Docker to create a communication bridge. The host's mapped port serves as a gateway, directing traffic to and from the container's internal port. Users can access a web application running within a container using the host's IP address on port 80 if, for example, the application listens on port 3000 and this port is mapped to port 80 on the host. This is true even though the program actually runs on port 3000 inside its container.

The principles of port mapping in Docker are simple and adaptable. Port mapping is made easier when a container is run with the -p flag when using the docker run command. -p 80:3000, where 80 is the host port and 3000 is the container port, is an example of a standard syntax. By using this mapping, any communication destined for port 80 on the host system will always find its way to port 3000 within the container. Here, Docker's flexibility really shows since it enables several mappings of this kind, meeting the needs of applications with diverse communication requirements. Additionally, Docker's dynamic nature allows various containers to map their internal ports to multiple host ports, guaranteeing that any containerized application is still reachable.

While port mapping handles communication, volume mapping deals with a distinct, yet equally important, issue: data persistence. By nature, containers are transient. As long as the container is in use, so are their file systems. Any information or state modifications within a container disappear when it is removed. This impermanence is unacceptable for a lot of applications, particularly databases or services that deal with user-generated content. They need a way to keep data alive through container restarts and terminations. Volume mapping provides an answer. Docker guarantees that any data written to a directory or file inside the container stays on the host, regardless of the container's lifespan, by mapping that directory or file to a place on the host system.

Docker volume mapping is a combination of accuracy and ease of use. This is achieved when running a container with the -v or --volume flag. A typical command may consist of -v /host/path:/container/path, where /host/path is the location on the host system, and /container/path is the target location inside the container. Any data written by the container to /container/path is, in nature, stored on /host/path on the host. Because of this symbiosis, data on the host is preserved and accessible by subsequent container instances, even in the event that the container gets stopped or removed. Docker further extends its adaptability by introducing named volumes, which abstract the actual storage location on the host, enabling Docker to manage the lifecycle of the volume.

When you think about it, Docker's port and volume mapping functions as lifelines that link the isolated world of containers to the vast host system and beyond. By ensuring port mapping, isolated applications running inside containers can communicate, providing users and collaborating with other services. On the other hand, volume mapping anchors these transient containers to the permanence of the host file system, guaranteeing data longevity.

In conclusion, port and volume mapping principles serve as pillars supporting this paradigm change as the digital environment rapidly adopts containerization. Their purpose is to guarantee that applications maintain their communicative and persistent qualities—qualities that are crucial for any real-world application—even when they benefit from isolation, consistency, and portability. Developers and system administrators may fully utilize Docker by skillfully handling port and volume mappings. This will allow them to create not just consistent and isolated applications but also interactive, robust, and always relevant in the ever-changing digital landscape.

**Managing container lifecycle**

The lifecycle management of applications is crucial in the software industry since these are constantly changing entities. The lifecycle of the container and the application it contains become the same when these applications are containerized with the aid of programs like

Docker. From the moment of creation until retirement, every stage of a container's life requires care, comprehension, and skillful handling. This section explores the nuances of the Docker container lifecycle and recommended practices for managing them, going deep into the topic.

Often hailed as lightweight virtual machines, Docker containers have completely changed how programs are created, deployed, and distributed. Applications are encapsulated in these containers together with their dependencies, guaranteeing isolation and consistency. However, these containers have a lifetime, just like any other living thing; there is a birth, an active existence, a possible dormant phase, and finally, an end.

A container's creation is its birth. A Docker image is used as the blueprint for a new container that is instantiated using the docker create command. Still, this new container is inactive, like a car that has been put together but not yet started. It takes up room but does nothing. One special benefit of this development step is that it gives you a chance to personalize and set up the container before it activates. This step allows developers to customize the container environment by mapping ports and volumes, changing network settings, and establishing environment variables.

The container needs to be given life after configuration in order to go from a dormant to an active state. To accomplish this, use the docker start command. Once started, the container takes on life of its own, with the encapsulated application operating and prepared to respond to queries or carry out specified functions. This stage, which is frequently the lengthiest in a container's lifespan, is when the application provides value by handling data processing, web page serving, or transaction facilitation.

Continuous operation isn't always required or desirable, though. In certain cases, such as while doing maintenance, updates, or resource optimization, a container's operation may need to be momentarily stopped. The docker pause and docker stop commands in Docker make this possible. Docker stop gently ends a container's processes and returns it to a dormant state, whereas docker pause momentarily freezes a container, maintaining its state but halting its execution. These commands guarantee that containers continue to be elastic entities that can adjust to changing operational needs.

However, what occurs when a container fulfills its function and is no longer needed? Here, the removal of the container completes the lifecycle. A container can be retired with the docker rm command, freeing up the resources it was using. But this goal isn't always definitive. Due to Docker's architecture, a container can be reincarnated, if necessary, since even if it is removed, the image from which it originated stays intact. Because of this cyclical structure, even though individual container instances may disappear, the possibility of them existing forever is guaranteed.

Although this lifecycle seems simple, managing it is not without its difficulties. Think about scale. In a development setting, several containers may be handled. In production, though, the size might be in the thousands or hundreds. Automation and technologies beyond basic Docker commands are required to orchestrate the lifespan of so many containers. Solutions like Kubernetes, Docker Swarm, and Docker Compose have evolved to solve this. Multi-container applications can be defined and executed with Docker Compose, which guarantees that containers with dependencies are managed simultaneously. On the other hand, container orchestration solutions like Kubernetes and Docker Swarm ensure that container lifecycles are managed effectively at scale, balancing loads, guaranteeing high availability, and enabling updates without downtime.

Monitoring is also essential to lifecycle management. When used with visualization platforms such as Grafana, tools such as Prometheus offer insights into resource utilization, health, and performance of containers. These are crucial insights that guide decisions about optimization, scaling, and troubleshooting.

When you stop to think about it, the lifecycle of a Docker container is a journey from creation to removal. With its own characteristics, difficulties, and possibilities, every stage necessitates understanding and skillful handling. Understanding the lifecycle of containers becomes strategic rather than merely a technical requirement as they become more commonplace. It ensures that applications interact, grow, and provide value even when contained within containers.

In conclusion, applications play crucial roles in the dynamic stage that is the digital landscape. Performance, availability, and evolution of these applications become intrinsically tied to the lifecycle of their containers when they are containerized. By skillfully managing this lifecycle, developers and operations teams can guarantee optimal application performance and lay the groundwork for continual value delivery, innovation, and agility in a dynamic digital ecosystem.

# CHAPTER VI

## Docker Compose

**Introduction to multi-container applications**

Software programs have changed from being simple, monolithic structures to complex, networked systems of interconnected services in today's dynamic digital environment. This progression highlights a paradigm change toward decentralized architectures and microservices, in which separate parts of a program operate independently but interact with each other without difficulty. Multi-container applications, in which each service operates in its own container while cooperating with others, are an expression of this change. This section explores the field of multi-container applications, including their history, importance, and the fundamental ideas that direct their design.

Software development was once dominated by monolithic architectures. Every functionality, including database management, data processing, and user interfaces, was controlled by a single codebase. Although the simplicity and consistency of this approach were positives, there were drawbacks as well, particularly with larger and more complicated applications. It got more and more difficult to scale certain features, execute upgrades without breaking the entire application, or isolate problems. The microservices paradigm was born out of the requirement for an architecture that was more resilient, scalable, and modular.

An application can be divided into smaller, independent services using microservices architecture, each of which can be created, deployed, and scaled independently. Every service is in charge of a certain functionality, and they all interact with one another through established protocols and APIs. Although there are many benefits to decentralization, it also presents a problem in managing these separate services, particularly when they must operate in isolated environments. Explore the realm of containers, with a focus on applications that utilize many containers.

Technologies such as Docker serve as examples of containers, which bundle dependencies with services and encapsulate them in isolated contexts. Consistency, portability, and isolation are guaranteed by this encapsulation. Nevertheless, the orchestration of these containers becomes essential when an application consists of several of these services, each operating in a separate container. In order to create a seamless multi-container application, this orchestration makes sure that containers find each other, communicate, share data, and scale in unison.

The granularity of control provided by multi-container applications is a key benefit. Different technologies can be used to design, scale, and update individual containerized services without affecting the others. For example, a web application may operate its database, front end, and back end in several containers. While the Python-built backend analyzes data and stores it in the database, which is an instance of MongoDB, the JavaScript-developed frontend manages user interactions. All these components are independent in terms of scalability, communication, and failure recovery.

The orchestrated symphony of multi-container applications, rather than their modularity, is what gives them their actual power. Because separate containers must find and connect with one another, it is critical to have tools and platforms that make this orchestration possible. For example, Docker Compose enables developers to describe services, networks, and volumes in a straightforward YAML file to construct multi-container applications. A program as a whole, with its network of connected containers, activates with a single command.

Although Docker Compose works well in local development environments, more reliable methods are needed when coordinating multi-container applications in production. This problem is addressed by the potent container orchestration tool Kubernetes. It guarantees the robustness and high availability of containers in addition to handling their deployment and scaling. Service discovery, load balancing, and automated rollouts are just a few of the capabilities that make Kubernetes a shining example for managing intricate multi-container systems in a variety of settings.

Gaining an understanding of the communication mechanisms that govern multi-container applications is also necessary. Each service operates independently, so how they exchange information, disseminate updates, or ask one another for tasks becomes essential.

This communication is made possible by protocols such as HTTP/REST, gRPC, or message brokers like RabbitMQ and Kafka. This ensures that services are segregated during execution yet stay interconnected during operation.

But immense power also entails great responsibility. Multi-container applications add complexity even if they provide scalability, flexibility, and durability. Developers and operations teams face issues involve dealing with network partitions, maintaining inter-container dependencies, protecting inter-service interactions, and ensuring consistent configurations. Teams are guided in navigating these obstacles by best practices, patterns, and principles such as the Twelve-Factor App methodology. This ensures that multi-container systems are not only functional but also secure, robust, and maintainable.

In conclusion, the requirement for durable, scalable, and modular applications develops as the digital tapestry becomes more complex. Answering this call are multi-container applications that combine the power of containerization with the concepts of microservices. They are a combination of development paradigms and operational procedures that guarantee software, in its ever-changing state, stays flexible, agile, and in step with the shifting currents of user requirements and technology breakthroughs. Instead of just creating software, developers and architects who are creating multi-container applications are composing a symphony of services that each contribute to the overall theme of digital transformation.

## Docker Compose basics

Different musical instruments are represented by separate containers in the digital symphony that is modern software development. Like an instrument, every container has a certain purpose. However, how can we make sure that these instruments blend together to produce a harmonious composition as opposed to a cacophony? Here comes Docker Compose, a conductor that combines several containers into a single application and manages its performance. In-depth discussion of Docker Compose's fundamentals, functions, and underlying ideas that underpin its orchestration magic are provided in this section.

Fundamentally, Docker Compose is a tool for creating and managing Docker applications that span several containers. Docker was originally focused on single-container operations, but its containerization capabilities transformed the software space by enabling applications and their dependencies to be encapsulated in isolated environments. On the other hand, real-world applications frequently consist of a number of linked services. Handling these services separately can be laborious and prone to mistakes, specifically when it comes to making sure they find and connect with one another. This problem is solved by Docker Compose, which gives developers the tools to define, configure, and manage several containers as a single, cohesive entity.

The docker-compose.yml file, a YAML-formatted configuration file where developers configure services, networks, and volumes for their application, is the central component of Docker Compose. Every service is associated with a container, and this file basically specifies the behavior, image to be used for construction, ports to be exposed, and communication between the container and other services that should occur within it. For example, in a standard web application architecture, there may be one service for the database, one for the backend API, and one for the web server. This one file has an organized definition of all these services and their connections as a result of Docker Compose.

Using Docker Compose to start an application is as easy as running the docker-compose up command. Using just one command, Docker Compose builds or gets the required images, starts the containers in the designated order, and consults the docker-compose.yml file to generate the required network and volume resources. Docker Compose's simplicity is its beauty; it removes the burden of initiating, linking, and maintaining numerous containers, freeing developers to concentrate on their application logic.

One of the main components of Docker Compose's orchestration capabilities is networking. All of the defined services (containers) are attached to a single default network that Docker Compose automatically sets up. The default configuration guarantees that services can locate and interact with each other with ease by using the hostnames defined for the services in the docker-compose.yml file. Furthermore, Docker Compose offers versatility by letting developers create unique networks that guarantee isolation or provide unique communication channels as needed.

Volumes are an essential component of Docker Compose that enable data sharing and persistence between containers. Volumes are essential for transferring configuration files between services and preserving database data during container restarts. Developers can specify named volumes, bind mounts, or even temporary volumes (tmpfs) in the docker-compose.yml file according to the data requirements of the application. The ability to store and share data at such a fine level highlights Docker Compose's skill at handling multi-container applications.

Growing applications require scaling by nature. This need is recognized by Docker Compose, which gives developers the ability to scale particular services. The number of container instances for a particular service can be readily increased or decreased by using the docker-compose up --scale command. The networking characteristics of Docker Compose in conjunction with this scaling capability guarantee that the underlying infrastructure can adjust dynamically to the growing demands of the applications.

It's important to remember that although Docker Compose performs exceptionally well in testing and development settings, production deployments are not part of its architecture. More capable orchestration solutions, like Kubernetes, are required because of the inherent difficulties of production, which range from complicated networking and security requirements to high availability and load balancing. However, before launching their multi-container applications into production environments, developers may define, test, and refine them in a beneficial environment provided by Docker Compose.

When all is said and done, Docker Compose is a testament to the Docker ethos: it makes difficult things simple. Although containers revolutionized the packaging and distribution of programs, Docker Compose takes this change a step further by guaranteeing that multi-container applications become cohesive units rather than complex puzzles. Docker Compose gives developers the tools they need to define, manage, and orchestrate services with ease. This gives them the confidence and precision to craft applications.

In conclusion, as the digital world develops, simplifying tools become indispensable. With its emphasis on coherence and simplicity, Docker Compose stands out as one such tool, coordinating the movement of containers and making sure that each service and container in the vast symphony of software applications operates in unison, enhancing the user experience. In this art form, Docker Compose creates an orchestrated performance that combines elegance and efficiency in addition to acting as conductor and choreographer.

## Writing and managing docker-compose.yml files

The design for multi-container applications that Docker Compose orchestrates is found in the docker-compose.yml file. The way an experienced architect creates blueprints to guarantee the perfect building of a large building, so too a developer meticulously constructs the docker-compose.yml file to specify the actions, interactions, and coordination of a group of containers. This section explores the craft of generating and maintaining these essential YAML files, highlighting their structure, importance, and best practices that highlight their efficient use.

In essence, Docker Compose makes the process of deploying multi-container applications less complicated. The docker-compose.yml file, a declarative configuration file that clarifies an application's composition, is essential to this simplicity. Developers can combine all of the application configuration into this one file, from which Docker Compose extracts instructions to launch the application, rather than having to use numerous Docker commands to manage separate containers.

Knowing the anatomy of a live thing is similar to knowing the structure of a docker-compose.yml file. At the top level, the file is divided into discrete parts, each of which deals with a particular aspect of the program. Without a doubt the most important part, the services section lists each of the separate containers that make up the application. Every service is associated with a container and contains information about the container to be created, including the Docker image, environment variables, networks, and volumes to be accessed. For example, services corresponding to web servers, databases, and cache layers may be found in a typical web application, all of which are set up to work well together.

The docker-compose.yml file serves the container's surrounding ecosystem in addition to services. While the volumes section handles data sharing and persistence, allowing containers to store or share data across lifecycles, the networks portion permits the construction of customized networks, facilitating complex communication channels between services. Despite being less frequently used, the secrets section is essential to security-conscious applications because it provides a safe way to handle sensitive data without exposing it inside the container.

Creating a docker-compose.yml file that works requires following a few guidelines. First and foremost, clarity is key. The maintainability of this file is ensured by its clear and well-commented structure, as developers will frequently review it for revisions. Making use of YAML's built-in reference system can reduce duplication and result in files that are easier to read and manage. Second, it's critical to comprehend the differences between build and image directives inside a service. The image directive just utilizes an already-existing Docker image, whereas the build directive points to a Dockerfile directory, instructing Docker Compose to build an image. Developers should carefully consider if they need a custom image or if a standard one would do.

The versioning of docker-compose.yml files is an important feature. Several iterations of the file format were required as Docker Compose developed and new capabilities were added. Compatibility and access to required features are guaranteed when the relevant version is specified at the beginning of the file. It is important for developers to keep abreast of version changes and adopt newer versions to take advantage of improved features while maintaining backward compatibility.

Writing environment-specific configurations for docker-compose.yml files is one of the aspects that is frequently disregarded. Although the main file may be optimized for a development environment, deployments to testing, staging, or production environments frequently result in differences. This requirement is met by Docker Compose's "override files" and "extension fields." Using the docker-compose -f command, developers can overlay numerous configuration files to create a modular and environment-specific setup by extracting common configurations into distinct files.

Especially in larger projects with several microservices, managing docker-compose.yml files require a deliberate approach. Using tools like Git to version control these files guarantees change tracking and promotes developer cooperation. Furthermore, it may be wise to divide configurations into several Compose files, each addressing a logical part of the application, as applications grow and new services are added. This modular strategy improves readability while providing more flexibility for controlling and deploying individual application components.

In conclusion, the foundation of Docker Compose orchestrated applications lies in the seemingly simple docker-compose.yml file. It's evidence of the effectiveness of declarative configurations, which make it simple for developers to articulate complex application setups. Writing and maintaining docker-compose.yml files requires an understanding of the intricacies that will become crucial as Docker and containerization continue to transform the software landscape. Ultimately, inside the extensive orchestra of containerized applications, this file serves as the outcome, directing every container and service to play in unison and produce a melodic tune that is efficient, scalable, and refined.

# CHAPTER VII

## Networking in Docker

### Understanding Docker's networking model

It is indisputable that Docker has advanced software development and deployment, revolutionizing the packaging, shipping, and operation of programs. The Docker container, an enclosed, self-sufficient environment where applications run, is at the center of this revolution. However, in order for these containers to function as intended, they require a strong networking model that enables them to interact with the host computer, other containers, and external devices. Docker's networking approach accomplishes this exact goal in a complex yet flexible way. This section explores the depths of the networking model provided by Docker, explaining its methods, nuances, and the mystery of seamless container communication.

Fundamentally, the networking strategy of Docker is about allowing containers to communicate in a variety of situations. Docker's networking model takes care of all of this, whether it's two containers on the same host that need to exchange data, a container that has to access the internet, or even an external device connecting to a container. This flexibility is accomplished by using a layered strategy, in which various network drivers address various communication contexts.

The 'bridge network' is one of the fundamental ideas of Docker's networking approach. The bridge network creates a private internal network on the host system by default when a Docker container is built, and it gives IP addresses to containers within its private range. Because of their private nature, containers can freely communicate with each other inside the same bridge network, but they will stay cut off from outside sources unless specific port mappings are set up. It's like having free-flowing conversations in separate chambers within a big mansion, yet needing a window (port) to let in outside noise.

For the majority of standalone containers, the bridge network is adequate; however, more intricate, multi-container applications really showcase Docker's networking prowess. Here is where the "overlay network" comes in, enabling containers dispersed over several host computers in a Docker Swarm to easily communicate as though they were on a single server. Developers can make sure that containers can easily locate and communicate with one other, regardless of where their hosts are located, by setting up an overlay network and adding services to it. This is Docker's solution to the problems that distributed systems present, making sure that the great distance of physical separation dissolves and is replaced by a seamless virtual environment.

Nevertheless, there are situations in which containers may have to share the host's networking stack in order to avoid going through the virtual network layer. Navigate to the "host network." In this mode of operation, a container accesses the host's networking namespace directly, giving the impression that its processes are executing on the host. Although isolation is compromised, this may be helpful for applications that require high performance and where network overhead should be kept to a minimum.

However, Docker's networking paradigm extends beyond pre-established network types. Docker introduced the notion of "network plugins" in recognition of the many requirements of contemporary applications. By enabling third-party tools and systems to integrate their own unique network types into Docker, these plugins offer specialized networking solutions catered to particular requirements.

Docker's networking model reflects the company's dedication to security. To give containers a MAC address and have them appear as physical devices on the network, use the'macvlan network'. When legacy applications are expecting to interface with physical hardware, this is extremely helpful. However, by providing the 'ipvlan' option within macvlan, Docker offers an additional degree of security, guaranteeing that containers can share the same IP address, port, and MAC address without interfering with one another.

Moreover, consideration should be given to the way DNS interacts with Docker's networking architecture. In user-defined networks, Docker's integrated DNS server helps containers resolve each other's names to their corresponding IP addresses. This makes it easier to discover services, which is a problem that microservices systems frequently face. Containers can find and communicate with one other simply by referencing the service name, abstracting away the complexity of IP management.

Digging deeper, load balancing and IP Address Management (IPAM) are two more issues that are addressed by Docker's networking strategy. While Docker's built-in load balancing distributes incoming requests to containers, guaranteeing optimal resource utilization and responsiveness, IPAM guarantees the methodical assignment, administration, and reuse of IP addresses.

In conclusion, Docker's networking paradigm offers a solution for almost any possible container communication scenario due to its versatile design. It strikes a balance between isolation and connectivity, giving containers the freedom to interact when needed and protection from unauthorized external access. Docker's networking strategy is a testament to its innovative approach, which understands the complex requirements of contemporary applications and provides elegant yet resilient solutions, as it continues to solidify its place as the cornerstone of containerization. Developers may create the perfect communication environment in the world of containers using Docker's networking, which offers a canvas of possibilities ranging from the quiet seclusion of the bridge network to the vast interconnectedness of the overlay.

## Bridge, host, and overlay networks

In an effort to simplify the development, deployment, and operation of applications, Docker has brought forward a number of innovative solutions to challenging technological problems. One such difficulty that is both significant and frequently overlooked is networking.

Three different types of networks exist within Docker's extensive networking capabilities: overlay, host, and bridge networks. Every one of these networks has a distinct function, supporting particular application designs and scenarios. We explore the details of these three networks in this section, shedding light on their features, uses, and underlying orchestration.

The "bridge network" is the most basic level of Docker networking. This bridge network is what is thought of as the default Docker network; whenever a container spins up without a defined network type, it immediately connects to it. From a conceptual standpoint, the bridge network operates similarly to a host system's private internal subnet. By obtaining their IP addresses from a range that is only available to the bridge network, containers linked to this network are essentially isolated from other networks. With this isolation, communication between containers on the same bridge network is guaranteed to be secure and seamless, and no unauthorized external parties can access the system unless specifically allowed. One of the bridge network's strengths is its inherent privacy. However, port mappings are useful when external communication is needed. Clearly defined by the developer, these mappings serve as conduits, connecting the host machine's designated ports to the internal container ports, closing the communication gap between the internal and external domains.

Isolation within the host machine is provided by the bridge network, but there are situations in which it may be detrimental. The 'host network' becomes the best option for applications that require direct communication with the host's networking environment without the need for Docker's virtual network as an intermediary layer. A container shares the host's complete networking namespace when it is operating in host mode. As a result, the networking stacks of the host and container are identical. Such a configuration has two benefits. Initially, it reduces network overhead, guaranteeing the smooth operation of applications with high performance demands. Second, without the extra layer of Docker's network abstraction, it provides simplicity in situations when the container needs to be tightly integrated with the host's networking configuration. But this open communication and lack of isolation can also be a double-edged sword, raising possible security issues.

As we move beyond single-host scenarios and into the domain of distributed applications running over many Docker hosts, we come across the concept of the "overlay network." Overlay networks are expressly made to support many hosts, particularly when using Docker Swarm mode. They act as a network bridge between containers that are operating on several Docker hosts. In order to do this, a virtual network that connects each Docker node taking part in the Swarm is created. No matter where they are physically located, containers can easily connect with each other within this large network just like they would if they were on the same local network. The traffic between containers is encapsulated by the overlay network using sophisticated techniques like VXLAN tunneling, which guarantees that the traffic is isolated and secure even while it is moving through external networks. Furthermore, the overlay network's integrated service discovery capability makes sure that containers can quickly locate and connect with one another using service names, abstracting the difficulties associated with IP management and container location. To put it simply, the overlay network presents a patchwork of dispersed containers as a unified, cohesive ecosystem.

When the three networks are combined, the principles of simplicity, scalability, and flexibility of Docker's vision become apparent. With its own private sanctum, the bridge network offers containers a safe refuge where their operations are unaffected by outside forces. In contrast, the host network creates a link between the host and the container, enabling them to share a single networking space in situations where deep integration and performance are critical. Furthermore, the overlay network's wide reach unites a disparate group of dispersed containers to form a single, cohesive environment in which time and space are irrelevant.

In conclusion, the bridge, host, and overlay networks created by Docker represent the flexibility of Docker's networking approach. With its own set of features, each form of network tackles a different set of issues, making Docker flexible enough to handle a wide range of application situations, whether they involve a single-container configuration on a single host or a multi-container application spread across a fleet of machines. With these three networks, Docker demonstrates its dedication to giving developers strong, user-friendly tools that let them design the networking environment that best fits the requirements of their applications. The way that Docker is reshaping software deployment and evolving with it is evidence of its creativity and insight in its complex approach to networking.

## Container-to-container communication

Docker has become a maestro in the vast digital symphony of software deployment, arranging complex movements and guaranteeing seamless operation. In this symphony, containers—individual performers—are the atomic components that execute particular duties, enabling the music to be more broadly composed. The way that containers communicate to one another is a crucial component of this orchestration. The arrangement as a whole would falter and the music would be discordant if there was ineffective communication between the containers. This section explores the subtleties of container-to-container communication in the Docker ecosystem, highlighting the approaches, difficulties, and orchestration strategies that control these exchanges.

The idea of isolation lies at the core of Docker's design philosophy. Fundamentally, each container is an isolated environment that protects the processes operating inside from outside interference. While this isolation guarantees security and steady performance, inter-container communication is hindered. What are some ways that design isolation might help containers work together harmoniously and support the seamless operation of multi-container applications? The answers lie in the complex and intricate networking mechanism of Docker.

When containers launch, they are connected to certain Docker networks. Because these networks are virtual, they control the communication between containers. Containers are placed on the bridge network, which is the default network unless otherwise noted. Containers on this network are able to communicate to one other through IP addresses. On the other hand, containers on various bridge networks stay separated and are unable to communicate with one another directly. By isolating several bridge networks, it prevents containers linked to distinct programs from unintentionally interfering with one another.

Docker provides user-defined networks for applications that require complex inter-container communication patterns. User-defined bridge networks provide more features than the default bridge network, such as automated DNS resolution. This adds ease and clarity to inter-container interactions by enabling containers on the same user-defined network to communicate not only through IP addresses but also using container names.

The overlay network becomes relevant when stepping into more complicated orchestration scenarios, particularly when there are numerous Docker hosts and containers involved. Overlay networks, created with Docker Swarm in mind, connect containers running on many hosts. Regardless of where they are physically located, containers can interact with each other effortlessly just like they would on the same local network thanks to the overlay network. Substantial methods such as VXLAN tunneling are used in the background to maintain the security and effectiveness of communication.

But communication between containers isn't limited to the networks they are connected to. It also entails keeping data integrity, guaranteeing synchronization, and regulating data flow. For example, in microservices architectures, containers are frequently used to represent discrete services that need to communicate with each other in real time, sharing information and handling requests. Because of this, it is necessary to employ protocols and standards that enable containers to send and receive data in predictable and structured ways. Furthermore, difficulties occur when data consistency or state maintenance are required of containers. These issues are frequently handled by using solutions like distributed databases, message queues, and caching algorithms, which guarantee that data transfers between containers proceed without interruption even in case of network failures or latency.

It gets even more complicated when you take container orchestration tools such as Kubernetes into account. Pods—groups of one or more containers—interact with one another within these platforms via services. By abstracting the underlying container IPs, these services offer a reliable endpoint for communication between pods. Every pod in the Kubernetes networking concept has its own IP address, and every container in a pod has access to the same local network. This architecture provides mechanisms for inter-pod communication within the larger cluster, while also guaranteeing simple inter-container communication within the same pod.

When communicating from one container to another, security is crucial. There's always a possibility of data breaches or unwanted access when data moves between containers. Network policies and firewall rules that control which containers can connect with one another are how Docker tackles these issues. Potential attackers are deterred by Docker's strict constraints, which guarantee that only authorized containers can share data.

In conclusion, Docker's container-to-container communication is a sophisticated and nuanced field with many facets. Docker provides tools and techniques that guarantee seamless communication between containers, from selecting the best network type to controlling data flow, guaranteeing synchronization, and upholding security. Knowing the nuances of inter-container communication becomes essential as multi-container systems continue to rule the software landscape. Docker's sophisticated networking infrastructure and security measures ensure that the performance continues without a discordant note. Container communication is crucial to the symphony of software deployment that is Docker.

# CHAPTER VIII

# Persistent Storage

## Importance of persistent storage

Docker's entrance into the software development and deployment space has completely changed the way programs are developed, deployed, and run. The idea of containerization, which is the packaging of software and its dependencies into discrete units to ensure consistent behavior across diverse contexts, is at the core of this growth. Although there are many advantages to using Docker containers, such as consistency, efficiency, and mobility, there is one drawback: the data in these containers is transient. This section explores the critical role that persistent storage plays in Docker, explaining why it's important, what problems it solves, and how important it is to the larger container ecosystem.

By design, Docker containers are transient. This implies that all data created or kept within a container is lost upon termination or restart. Although this temporary nature is useful for preserving stateless systems, guaranteeing consistency, and making rollbacks simple, it presents difficulties when applications require long-term data storage and retrieval. Consider a complex file storage service or database system operating inside of a container. Any data entered into these systems would disappear upon container termination if persistent storage wasn't included, making them essentially useless for long-term applications.

This is the point where the idea of persistent storage becomes essential. When we talk about systems that enable data to survive the lifecycle of individual containers, we're talking about persistent storage. This means that data is preserved and easily available, regardless of the fleeting actions of the containers that generate or consume it. The whole purpose of persistent storage in Docker is to bridge the gap between the transient nature of containers and the constant need for data storage.

The easiest way to appreciate the significance of persistent storage in Docker is to think about actual application scenarios. Probably the most tangible examples are databases. The main purpose of any database, whether it's a NoSQL system like MongoDB or a relational database like PostgreSQL, is to store, retrieve, and manage data over time. The real data in a Dockerized environment needs to be stored in a persistent storage solution so that it may survive container restarts, failures, and migrations, even though the database software may run inside a container.

In addition to databases, a plethora of other applications require persistent storage. Think about file storage services, content management systems, or even caching techniques. Although the systems' operating logic can be contained in containers, the material itself—whether it be multimedia files, web pages, or cached data—needs to be permanent. These apps' whole purpose would be undermined by persistent storage, which would leave them in a constant state of data amnesia.

With regard to the requirement for persistent storage, Docker provides a number of integrations and techniques. For example, a native solution called Docker Volumes makes data persistence possible by enabling data to be kept outside of the container's file system. Docker volumes are separate entities from containers, so that data contained in the volume is preserved in the event that a container is removed. To further increase their usefulness, these volumes can be shared and repurposed across several containers.

Bind mounts are another method for achieving persistent storage in Docker. A particular file or directory on the host system is linked to a container through bind mounts. This ensures persistence by writing all data written by the container to this designated location directly to the host system. Although bind mounts are strong, their portability is limited compared to Docker Volumes because of their strong connection to the host's directory structure.

In more complex scenarios, Docker also effortlessly interfaces with external storage options, particularly in dispersed cloud-based architectures. Docker can be used to communicate with cloud storage platforms such as Google Persistent Disk and Amazon EBS. This gives containers the same capabilities as local storage but with the added advantages of scalability, redundancy, and global accessibility.

Though the underlying reasoning for persistent storage in Docker is straightforward—data is extremely valuable in the digital world—the mechanics of the feature are complex. Most modern applications rely on the persistent storage, management, and retrieval of data, be it analytical data, transactional records, configuration settings, or user-generated content. Docker's ability to support persistent storage expands its usefulness and brings its consistency and mobility concept into the data world.

In conclusion, Docker's capabilities go beyond simply containerizing applications; it can also be used to balance the transient and permanent aspects of software. Persistent storage in Docker is crucial for reasons that go beyond technical ones, including user experience, application dependability, and data continuity. Docker's persistent storage techniques make sure that data continues to play in the movement between software logic and data, even when containers come and leave.

## Volumes vs bind mounts

With its revolutionary approach to software distribution, the Docker world offers developers and system administrators a plethora of options to optimize workflows. One of the most important decisions is data persistence, or how and where to manage and store data to ensure that it endures the naturally short life of containers. Volumes and bind mounts are the two main technologies that make this data persistence in Docker possible. Both achieve the general objective of keeping data safe after the container's lifecycle, but they differ in how they work, how useful they are, and how subtle they are. This section aims to present a comprehensive analysis of volumes and bind mounts in Docker, clarifying their unique features, benefits, and suitable use cases.

To begin with, it's important to understand why data persistence techniques are required in the first place. By definition, Docker containers are temporary. When a container is terminated, any data created or saved inside its readable layer is lost. There are several advantages to this transient behavior, including preserving statelessness and enabling quick deployment. But when applications need data to survive container restarts, migrations, or failures—like file storage systems or databases—it becomes problematic. Docker provides a solution to this problem: introduce volumes and bind mounts.

Within the Docker context, volumes are specifically created storage spaces that exist apart from containers and their lifetime. Volumes, which are created and maintained by Docker itself, are stored in a portion of the host file system that Docker manages and is segregated from it (usually under /var/lib/docker/volumes). Volumes benefit from the separation from the host's file system. Initially, it removes the complexity of the host's underlying file system, increasing the portability and consistency of volumes between host settings. Because of this abstraction, Docker can also provide sophisticated functionalities like volume drivers, which let volumes be backed by cloud or external storage providers.

Furthermore, data longevity is guaranteed by the decoupling of volumes from containers. Volumes are independent of containers, so the data on them is unaffected even in the event that the container with it is terminated. Volumes are a great option for situations when data mobility and integrity are crucial, such databases or application configuration files, because of their resilience and independence.

Bind mounts are situated on the opposite end of the spectrum. Bind mounts are simply directories (or individual files) on the host file system that are directly mounted into a container, whereas volumes are Docker-managed entities living on Docker-managed portions of the host file system. A container that accesses a bind mount goes straight to the host's bind-mounted directory. There are benefits to this direct connectivity, but it also has its own set of complications.

The immediate nature of bind mounts is one of their main benefits. Changes made to the data inside the container are immediately reflected on the host and vice versa since bind mounts are direct mappings to the file system of the host. Because of this, bind mounts come in very handy when testing code or data on the host in a containerized environment without having to continuously rebuild container images throughout development stages.

Nonetheless, there are additional difficulties because of the close connection between bind mounts and the host's file system. Bind mounts are closely related to the subtleties and directory structure of the host, in contrast to the abstraction offered by volumes. Because of their close association, bind mounts are less adaptable to various host settings. Inconsistent behavior or problems may arise if a container that is anticipating a bind mount is transferred to a different host without the anticipated directory structure.

Moreover, the volume management tools of Docker are not useful for bind mounts. They lack the layer of isolation that Docker-managed volumes give, and they do not support volume drivers. This means that, even while bind mounts are effective in some situations, using them requires a deeper comprehension of the file system on the host as well as any possible ramifications of this direct association.

Volumes and bind mounts have different characteristics, thus which one to choose depends on the particular needs of the project. Volumes are ideal for production situations where data consistency, portability, and durability are crucial due to their Docker-managed nature, isolation from the host file system, and support for external storage drivers. However, bind mounts excel in development environments where quick iterations and direct access to host data are crucial due to their immediate nature and direct relationship to the file system.

In conclusion, exploring Docker's data persistence features—particularly volumes and bind mounts—reveals a world in which decisions are made based more on contextual appropriateness than on absolute superiority. Although they address various aspects of this objective, volumes and bind mounts both fulfill the general need of protecting data in a world of transient containers. As with many technological decisions, it's critical to comprehend the fundamental workings, advantages, and disadvantages of each alternative. Volumes and bind mounts provide distinct beats in the data and Docker dance, each one attractive in its own right and corresponding to a different stage of the software lifecycle.

## Managing and backing up data in Docker

Within the broad field of software development and deployment, Docker has become a shining example of consistency, efficiency, and agility. Undoubtedly, technology has completely changed the way applications are created, distributed, and used, but data management is still a constant concern. Since data is essential to many applications, it is crucial to make sure that it not only survives but also is properly handled and backed up in an environment where containers may be transient. This section explores best practices and approaches to guarantee data resilience and integrity, delving into the complexities of maintaining and backing up data in Docker.

It's important to comprehend the nature of Docker containers before anything else. By nature, containers are transient and stateless. When a container terminates, any data created inside its readable layer is removed. Applications that depend on persistent data have difficulties because of its transient nature, even while it is advantageous for maintaining consistency and clean states. Docker provides tools like volumes and bind mounts to ensure data persistence even after a container has ended, in recognition of this difficulty. Persistence is only the first step, though; more advanced techniques are needed for efficient data management.

Selecting one of Docker's data persistence technologies consciously is the first step toward data management. Volumes provide a layer of abstraction from the host filesystem because they are storage spaces that are handled by Docker. They take advantage of Docker's management features and are ideal for applications that need to transfer data between hosts. Bind mounts offer instant reflection between the host and container data because they map straight to the host disk. They are particularly helpful in the stages of development where rapid iterations are required. Through comprehension of the application's requirements and characteristics, developers can select the most suitable approach to initiate their data management endeavors.

After data durability is attained, the emphasis switches to keeping it organized. Having a well-organized volume naming standard can make data management much easier. Identification can be made easier by using names that are descriptive and reflect the function or use of a volume, particularly when working with a large number of volumes and containers. Moreover, Docker provides commands for volume removal, pruning, and inspection. Using these commands on a regular basis guarantees that unused or orphaned volumes—which can take up important disk space—are recognized and handled properly.

It becomes imperative to provide data resiliency beyond organization. Data resilience in the context of Docker mostly refers to backing up data that is kept on volumes or bind mounts. Frequent backups offer protection against unanticipated data loss as well as a fallback in the event of program problems or corrupted data.

Generally, backing up Docker volumes is a multi-step procedure. The volume that has to be backed up must first be mounted in a container. To complete the backup, this container can employ a base image that is lightweight and equipped with the required tools. Data can be compressed, archived, and then moved to a backup location—

a distant server, cloud storage, or even a local backup drive—once the container has started operating. This operation can be facilitated by using programs like tar or rsync, which take snapshots of the volume's contents.

Likewise, the procedure is basically the opposite for data restoration. Data can be extracted and restored after moving the backup archive to a container that mounts the target volume. It is essential to test this restoration procedure on a regular basis to make sure that backups are being made and that they are legitimate and recoverable.

Frequency is another aspect of backup plan. Backups can be scheduled on a weekly, daily, or even hourly basis, depending on the type of application and how frequently the data is changed. Differential or incremental backups, which only save the modifications made since the last backup and spare storage space, could also be useful for some applications.

Although the procedure mentioned above explains manual backups, efficiency depends on automation. Backup scripts can be scheduled using tools such as cron on Linux, which guarantees that backups are performed automatically on a regular basis. Furthermore, there are a number of third-party programs that focus on Docker data backups and offer functions like encryption, data deduplication, and automated backups.

In conclusion, Docker presents unmatched benefits for growing and deploying applications, but it also highlights the necessity of efficient data management. Making sure that data survives the brief lifecycle of containers is only the beginning. In Docker, true data management consists of automated tools and procedures that integrate systematic storage, frequent backups, and recurring restoration tests. As long as Docker is a vital component of today's software architecture, data management best practices and principles will be essential. Data is, after all, the constant in the dynamic dance of containers and applications; it is the rhythm that gives the music its meaning.

# CHAPTER IX

# Advanced Docker Tips and Tricks

## Docker best practices

Docker's introduction into the software industry changed everything by simplifying the development, deployment, and scaling of applications. Its containerized architecture offers developers the unprecedented benefit of generating consistent and reproducible environments. However, Docker's full potential can only be realized by using it with a sophisticated grasp of its best practices, just like any other tool. Utilizing Docker's full potential requires following these best practices, which range from improving performance and security to optimizing image builds. This section explores these practices in detail, emphasizing their importance and providing instructions on how to incorporate them into the Docker workflow.

The images that make up Docker's foundation are its blueprints for containers. One of the most important best practices is to optimize these images. A lighter image speeds up deployment and scaling in addition to cutting down on build time. The most precise base image, which has all the elements required for the application, should always be used. Narrowing down to a customized base image can heavily reduce the size, as opposed to beginning with a generic image that might include unnecessary software. Furthermore, bloat is avoided, and the image remains lean by grouping actions into a Dockerfile and cleaning up in the same layer, such as removing temporary files following an installation phase.

Given its critical role in today's digital world, security is a fundamental component of Docker best practices. To start, make sure to always download base images from reliable sources. For example, verified images are provided by the official Docker Hub, guaranteeing that they are devoid of dangerous components. To take advantage of patches and security updates, these images must be updated on a regular basis. Beyond the images, runtime security for containers also needs to be considered. Potential security risks are reduced when containers are run according to the least privilege principle, which grants them only the minimal amount of permissions necessary for operation. Additional security can be strengthened by mapping container processes to a non-root user on the host system using user namespaces.

Docker may be inherently isolated by design, but networking is where security holes may appear. By default, Docker containers can make unrestricted outbound connections. Using a customized bridge network and putting up firewall rules can restrict this, ensuring containers only communicate as and when necessary. Furthermore, sensitive information should never be hardcoded into Docker images, including API keys and database credentials. Using Docker secrets or environment variables guarantees this data remains protected and can be accessed safely by containers when required.

Efficiency in Docker also extends to resource management. Containers, by default, can consume infinite CPU and memory of the host machine. However, in multi-container setups in particular, this can result in resource contention. Setting resource limitations and reservations for CPU and RAM helps ensure that containers have the resources they require while avoiding any single container from monopolizing the system. This not only provides smoother performance but also promotes stability across the board.

Another key aspect is assuring data persistence and administration. Volumes and bind mounts are essential for data persistence because Docker containers are ephemeral. While doing so, one must also backup this data periodically, ensuring resilience against data loss or corruption. In addition, efficient log management guarantees that any problems or irregularities may be found and fixed right away. Logging from multiple containers can be easier to monitor, search, and analyze when using centralized logging solutions.

Lastly, the practice of continuous integration and continuous deployment (CI/CD) fits seamlessly with Docker. Applications are kept safe, up to current, and bug-free by automatically building images as part of the continuous integration process, executing automated tests in containers, and deploying them. Here, Docker's consistency is essential since it guarantees that the environment stays unchanged from development to production.

In conclusion, Docker is a strong tool, but achieving its full potential requires a methodical approach. As the lighthouse that leads developers and system administrators through the maze of options, best practices make sure applications continue to be scalable, safe, and effective. Everything from the fundamental process of image optimization to the more complex domains of resource management and security, each technique enhances the Docker experience. Following these best practices will be essential as the digital world relentlessly moves toward microservices and containerization, making sure that Docker stays more than just a tool—rather, a catalyst for software excellence.

## Security considerations

The software industry has unquestionably undergone a transformation with the rise of containerization, especially with the widespread use of Docker. Development and operations teams now have a more streamlined, reliable, and effective way to deploy applications due to containers. These advantages are not without difficulties, though, as is the case with any technical advancement. Security is one of the most important issues in a Docker ecosystem that needs to be addressed. If not sufficiently handled, a multitude of possible vulnerabilities can be exploited, ranging from the images that form the foundation of containers to the runtime environments and networks that these containers consume. This section explores the critical security aspects of Docker and highlights the significance of protecting containerized settings in the modern digital world.

At its foundation, Docker uses images to build containers. These images, which are frequently layered compositions of many software elements, may unintentionally carry security flaws. As a result, the first line of defense for Docker security is now the source of these images. It is crucial to always make sure that the images are retrieved from reliable and trustworthy archives. For example, confirmed images from the official Docker Hub guarantee that their contents have been thoroughly examined. It is crucial to update these images on a regular basis in order to apply updates and address known vulnerabilities, even when using reliable sources.

Obtaining secure images is a vital first step, but it's not the end. Examining the construction and customization of these images is also necessary. Security should be taken into consideration when creating Dockerfiles, which are scripts that specify how images are built. Important recommended practices include avoiding using the root user, reducing the number of installed components, and making sure that no sensitive information, such as passwords or API keys, is embedded in the image. Additionally, images can be scanned for vulnerabilities using programs like Docker Bench or Clair, which adds an extra degree of security checks prior to deployment.

Another crucial factor is runtime security. Docker containers,by default, are isolated from the host system and from one another. On the other hand, if containers are run with a lot of privileges, this isolation could be weakened. It is imperative to embrace the idea of least privilege, which states that a container should only be allowed the permissions that it truly requires. To ensure that even if a malicious entity gains access to a container, its potential to affect the underlying host system or other containers is limited, it is recommended to avoid running containers as the root user and to utilize user namespaces.

In a Dockerized environment, the network—which is frequently the lifeblood of applications—also presents potential security risks. By default, a bridge network is used by Docker to facilitate communication between containers. Although this makes it easier for containers to communicate with one another, if it's not configured properly, it may also expose containers to threats. These threats can be reduced by using more secure networking modes, such as overlay networks or custom bridge networks with firewall rules. Network segmentation, which limits communication between certain containers, can also strengthen security for particularly critical applications.

Data is another area where Docker security issues are important because it is the foundation of many modern applications. Because of Docker's ephemeral nature—data inside a container is lost when the container is destroyed—persistent storage requires the usage of volumes or bind mounts. Nonetheless, security shouldn't be jeopardized by this persistence. The key to ensuring that data is secure and durable is to make sure it is encrypted both while it is in transit and at rest, use volume plugins that add more security levels, and frequently backup your data.

Finally, the guardians of a safe Docker environment are monitoring and logging. By using real-time monitoring tools, one can gain insights into the behavior of containers and identify anomalies that might point to a security breach. Together with this, thorough log maintenance and tool analysis may guarantee that potential threats are promptly detected and dealt with.

In conclusion, security issues for Docker are becoming more and more important as it remains a foundation of contemporary software deployment processes. An all-encompassing approach to security is necessary, from the first stages of sourcing and generating images through the runtime concerns of networking, data processing, and permissions. The combination of best practices, tools, and a watchful mentality fortifies against potential threats, guaranteeing that the numerous advantages of Docker are reaped without compromising the security and integrity of applications. To ensure that containerized systems continue to serve as strongholds against malevolent organizations, Docker security presents a dynamic challenge in the always changing world of cyber threats. This requires regular updates, awareness campaigns, and proactive measures.

## Optimizing Docker for performance

Docker has become indispensable in the dynamic field of software development and deployment, enabling scalability, consistency, and portability. As more and more enterprises use Docker and containerization, it becomes critical to guarantee optimal performance. Docker is naturally efficient, but to fully profit from its architecture, you will need to learn and adjust its many components. This section explores the tactics and factors to take into account while optimizing Docker for performance, so that containerized applications function as smoothly, effectively, and efficiently as possible.

Images are the blueprints for containers and are at the core of the Docker architecture. The first step towards guaranteeing overall Docker performance is to optimize these images. Large images take longer to transfer and deploy, and they also use more storage. Therefore, performance can be greatly improved by producing lightweight images by using fewer base images, fewer layers, and less unnecessary files. By combining layers, tools such as docker-squash can help reduce the size of images. Moreover, the multi-stage build functionality enables developers to produce lean production images by removing build-time artifacts that are not needed.

Although image optimization is the cornerstone of performance tuning, it is as important to comprehend and manage container resources. When several containers run concurrently, resource contention may arise since a container's default behavior allows it to consume the whole CPU and memory of the Docker host. Administrators can restrict how much CPU and memory a container can utilize by launching it with the --cpus and --memory parameters. By preventing any one container from using up all the resources, these restrictions create a balanced environment where each container uses its fair amount of resources, improving performance overall.

Given that networking is the backbone of most modern applications, it requires extra care in a Dockerized environment. Although the bridge network mode by default in Docker is appropriate for several scenarios, it might not always be the best option in terms of performance. The host networking option, in which the container shares the host's network namespace, can provide better performance for applications that require high throughput. Additionally, the overlay network for swarm services can be adjusted using a variety of settings, such as customizing Maximum Transmission Units (MTUs) to minimize data packet sizes for the particular infrastructure. The overlay network enables communication between containers across multiple nodes.

Another important component of containerized applications is storage, which has its own set of performance requirements. Docker provides a number of storage drivers, each with unique performance characteristics, such as overlay2, aufs, and btrfs. Considerable performance gains might result from selecting the appropriate driver based on the application's I/O patterns. Furthermore, even though Docker volumes provide a practical means of data persistence, it's critical to comprehend how they affect performance. Direct host mounts, sometimes known as bind mounts, may perform better than named or anonymous volumes in data-intensive applications.

External factors influence Docker's performance in addition to its inherent components. The operating system and hardware of the underlying host can have a big impact on Docker's effectiveness. An optimal Docker environment can be achieved by making sure the host system is not resource-starved, updating the host OS and Docker daemon on a regular basis, and adjusting the host's kernel parameters. Administrators can find bottlenecks and opportunities for improvement in container performance by combining Grafana visualizations with monitoring tools like Prometheus or cAdvisor.

Finally, while maximizing performance is frequently the goal of performance optimization, stability and predictability are also important. A realistic understanding of the Docker environment's limitations can be obtained by routinely stress-testing it with tools like docker-stress or benchmarking tools. By ensuring that the system is resilient under stress, these tests help to prevent unexpected performance degradations in real-world production circumstances.

In conclusion, a new paradigm in software deployment is introduced by Docker's promise of consistency, scalability, and isolation. However, reaching its optimal potential necessitates a thorough comprehension of all of its constituent parts and how they affect performance. Docker's performance may be tuned to match complex application requirements through careful image management, resource allocation, network and storage tuning, and close observation of outside variables. Performance optimization makes sure that Docker not only changes the way applications are deployed but also ensures that they operate at their best, producing value in an efficient and effective manner, as containerization continues to rule the software landscape.

# CHAPTER X

# Docker in the DevOps Lifecycle

## Continuous Integration and Continuous Deployment (CI/CD) with Docker

The capacity to offer changes and upgrades quickly and consistently has become a key differentiator in today's agile and fast-paced software industry. The twin pillars of continuous integration (CI) and continuous deployment (CD), which have completely changed the way developers approach software creation, testing, and deployment, now come into play. A previously unthinkable era of streamlined software delivery is ushered in when CI/CD pipelines are paired with the capabilities of Docker, a platform created to assure consistency across different phases of the development lifecycle.

The process of regularly integrating code updates from various contributors into a central repository is known as continuous integration. The next step is to automatically test each integration in order to find faults and inconsistencies as soon as possible. While CI concentrates on integrating and validating changes swiftly, Continuous Deployment takes it a step further. Code updates are automatically pushed to the production environment by CD, provided they pass all required tests. The combined goals of CI and

CD are to minimize errors, decrease manual intervention, and expedite the software release process.

The addition of Docker to this ecosystem increases these advantages. Docker's containerization technology essentially allows software developers to package an application and its associated dependencies into a standardized unit for software development, ensuring consistency across various circumstances. This solves the "it works on my machine" issue, which is one of the most prevalent problems in software development. This consistency in CI/CD terms means that code that compiles and runs locally in a Docker container will continue to function the same way whether it is merged into the main branch, tested in a staging environment, or even put into production.

A number of software delivery process stages are significantly altered by the combination of Docker and CI/CD. Docker containers are a useful tool for developers to use when they want to replicate production-like settings on their workstations. As a result, there are fewer environment-specific disparities, which makes the integrated code more reliable and less prone to environment-specific bugs. Docker's rapid spin-up and tear-down of containers makes testing possible in parallel, which significantly cuts down on testing time. To guarantee that tests don't conflict with one another and that the findings are consistent, automated test suites might operate in separate containers for various software components.

Because staging and production environments differ, the deployment phase might be complicated. Docker's integration with CI/CD simplifies this process. By enclosing the application and its surroundings, containers guarantee that the exact same version of the application is deployed during continuous integration (CI). Post-deployment issues and deployment failures are significantly decreased by this uniformity. Furthermore, the deployment process may be made even more smooth and resilient by using orchestrators like Kubernetes, which provide autonomous deployment, scaling, and management of Docker containers.

Docker's benefits have been acknowledged by a number of CI/CD systems, including Jenkins, GitLab CI, and Travis CI, which provide excellent assistance in constructing pipelines based on Docker. By defining Docker-based build environments with these tools, developers can make sure that the CI/CD pipeline uses the same environment as the developers. In addition, Docker images may be created, maintained, and versioned as part of the continuous integration (CI) process, guaranteeing that the runtime environment and the application's code are both version-controlled and traceable.

Additionally, creating and packaging applications with Docker is becoming more and more popular. Developers can use Docker multi-stage builds in replacement of building applications on continuous integration (CI) servers and then containerizing the resultant artifacts. By using this method, developers may specify both the build and runtime environments in a single Dockerfile, guaranteeing that the application is constructed inside a container and producing a production-ready, lean container image. Ensuring an end-to-end containerized workflow, this image may then be pushed to a container registry as part of CI and deployed to production as part of CD.

Docker offers new concerns and problems in addition to enabling CI/CD. In a Docker-centric CI/CD configuration, container security, image versioning, and large-scale container orchestration management become critical tasks. With the correct procedures, resources, and knowledge of Docker's nuances, these difficulties can be successfully overcome.

In conclusion, the combination of Docker and CI/CD demonstrates how forward-thinking software engineering has evolved to produce dependable software at previously unheard-of speeds. Docker is a crucial component of the CI/CD process since it guarantees consistency, reproducibility, and portability. Docker integration is not only a creative solution, but also a must for enterprises looking to maintain their competitiveness in the rapidly evolving digital market. Developers and organizations are better prepared to manage the difficulties of modern software delivery through continuous integration, testing, deployment, and the consistent environments offered by Docker. This ensures that they can quickly and reliably bring their innovations to the world.

## Integrating Docker with popular CI/CD tools

Enhancing speed, reliability, and efficiency is the constant goal of the ever-evolving software development industry. This goal has been made possible in large part by two essential components: Docker and Continuous Integration/Continuous Deployment (CI/CD) techniques. Although each of these technologies is potent on its own, their combined effect is genuinely revolutionary. In-depth discussion of Docker's integration with a number of well-known CI/CD systems and its significant effects on contemporary software delivery processes are provided in this section.

The core functionality of Docker is its ability to containerize applications, which encapsulates them along with their necessary dependencies in a uniform environment. This guarantees consistent application operation regardless of the Docker container's deployment location, be it the production server, a testing environment, or the developer's workstation. This uniformity has the direct effect of significantly lowering the infamous "it works on my machine" phenomenon. Knowing that there won't be any unforeseen inconsistencies allows the same application container that was developed and tested during the integration phase to be reliably deployed to production in the context of CI/CD.

Numerous CI/CD tools have benefited from Docker's advantages. Jenkins, GitLab CI, Travis CI, CircleCI, and GitHub Actions are a few of the well-known ones. Although Docker has been integrated into each of these solutions in a different way, the general idea is always the same: using Docker to guarantee a dependable, effective, and simplified CI/CD pipeline.

With numerous plugins that facilitate Docker integration, Jenkins, one of the most well-known open-source automation servers, is readily integrated. 'Docker agents' can be defined by developers using Jenkins to conduct builds within Docker containers. By doing this, you can be sure that the build environment is always consistent and that the current build won't be impacted by any residuals from earlier builds. Furthermore, Docker images may be created, tests can be conducted inside containers, and verified images can be pushed to Docker registries using custom Jenkins pipelines.

Docker is ingrained in the design of GitLab CI, a component of the larger GitLab ecosystem. In the '.gitlab-ci.yml' configuration file, GitLab CI enables the definition of Docker images as the operating environment for CI jobs. Moreover, building, storing, and deploying Docker images within the GitLab environment is made simple by the integrated GitLab Container Registry.

Developers can designate Docker as a service in the '.travis.yml' file to enable Docker-based builds with the help of Travis CI, a cloud-based CI/CD tool. This means that in order to ensure that the build and tests execute in a containerized environment, Travis CI will spin up the necessary Docker containers during the build process.

Another well-known cloud-based CI/CD platform, CircleCI, highlights the importance of Docker to its processes. '.circleci/config.yml', the main configuration file for CircleCI, allows developers to define several tasks, each of which runs in a different Docker image. This expedites the build-test-deploy cycle by enabling parallelism and ensuring consistency. Multiple jobs can execute concurrently in their own containers.

Relatively new to the CI/CD space but quickly gaining traction, GitHub Actions provides excellent support for Docker. Developers can create workflows inside GitHub repositories that generate Docker images, launch tests within Docker containers, and submit images to container registries such as GitHub's own GitHub

Container Registry or Docker Hub. GitHub Actions provides a highly straightforward way for projects hosted on GitHub to implement Docker-based CI/CD pipelines.

While there are many benefits to integrating Docker with these CI/CD systems, there are also some possible drawbacks that should be considered. It is essential to make sure that Docker images are lightweight, secure, and appropriate for the work at hand. Many frequent difficulties can be mitigated by regularly checking images for security vulnerabilities, using official base images, and reducing the number of image layers.

In conclusion, the way that Docker integrates with well-known CI/CD systems is a symbol of the larger movement in software development toward consistency, dependability, and speed. Docker's synergy with CI/CD tools offers a compelling solution to developers who want to deliver value faster without compromising quality. The needs of modern software delivery, which are defined by rapid iterations, agility, and high reliability, can be met by development teams by encapsulating applications within Docker containers and utilizing CI/CD solutions that natively support Docker's features. Thus, this fusion symbolizes not just a technological integration but also a harmonization of processes and principles that shape software development going forward.

## Docker in production environments

Docker has made an undeniable revolutionary impact on the software development industry. Docker began out as a tool to make the process of developing and testing applications easier. Over time, it developed into a strong platform that could manage the demands and complexity of production settings. The use of Docker in production signifies a paradigm shift in the packaging, deployment, and scaling of software—rather than merely an incremental improvement in deployment techniques. This section explores the compelling factors that led to Docker's ascent to prominence as a production-grade solution, as well as the things that businesses need to think about when making the transition to containerized deployments.

The main attraction of Docker for production settings is its assurance of consistency. With Docker, the notorious "it works on my machine" problem—which has historically plagued operations and development teams alike—virtually disappears. By encapsulating the program and all of its dependencies, containers guarantee that the program will function the same way anywhere it is executed. This implies that production can safely utilize the same Docker image that was used for development and testing without worrying about environment-specific differences.

In addition, Docker containers are less heavy than conventional virtual machines (VMs). Containers are substantially faster to start up and have a lot smaller footprint because they share the host system's kernel instead of simulating a whole operating system. Better infrastructure utilization results from this, enabling the execution of more applications on the same hardware without compromising performance. In production contexts, this kind of efficiency is essential, especially when scaling out to handle higher loads.

Docker containers' transient nature offers an alternative perspective on application state. This corresponds to stateless application design in production, where any required state is saved in external services or databases. Easy horizontal scalability is made possible by this design philosophy; more instances of the program can be spun up quickly in response to demand increase without requiring complex synchronization or state management issues.

Adopting Docker in a production environment is not without its difficulties, though. Different from standard deployments, networking, storage, and monitoring are areas that frequently call for further consideration. Fortunately, Docker's thriving ecosystem has led to the development of solutions that address these issues. The orchestration of many containers, handling of networking between containers, guaranteeing high availability, and scaling out applications based on demand are made easier by tools such as Docker Compose, Docker Swarm, and Kubernetes.

Another critical topic to focus on when implementing Docker in production is security. A vulnerability in one container may be exploited to impact the host or other containers because they share the same kernel. Docker has addressed these issues by adding features like seccomp profiles and user namespaces, which improve container isolation and lower the risk profile. Other suggested best practices include using minimum base images, checking images for known security concerns, and routinely upgrading Docker images to patch vulnerabilities.

Another typical difficulty is managing persistent data in a containerized system. Data should not be directly stored in containers because they are transient. To guarantee data persistence, Docker provides options like volumes and bind mounts. These storage solutions can be linked with distributed storage backends using orchestration tools, guaranteeing data availability and resilience.

The cultural and procedural adjustments that result from using Docker in production must also be taken into account. Teams working on development, operations, and security must closely coordinate, which frequently calls for a change to a DevOps culture. To make sure that processes are in line with the requirements of containerized deployments, they must be frequently reevaluated and often revamped.

In conclusion, even if Docker offers a compelling value proposition for production deployments, using it requires a thorough grasp of both its advantages and disadvantages. Docker offers unmatched consistency, efficiency, and scalability, revolutionizing software delivery and operation. To truly benefit from it, though, businesses need to make the investment to comprehend its nuances, modify their procedures, and make sure that their staff members are qualified to handle containerized applications. When all of these components come together, Docker may be a very effective solution that greatly improves an organization's software delivery capabilities and makes sure that it is efficient, adaptable, and ready to take on the constantly changing needs of the contemporary digital landscape.

# CHAPTER XI

# Kubernetes and Docker

## Introduction to Kubernetes

The desire for scalability, resilience, and efficient resource utilization has taken center stage in the constantly changing field of software development. A new problem arose with the advent of microservices architectures and the container revolution led by Docker: effectively managing, orchestrating, and scaling containers across a fleet of servers. Kubernetes is a potent container orchestration technology that tackles these issues and ushers in a new era of cloud-native applications for the software industry.

Drawing on their years of experience in running services at huge scale using a system called Borg, Google originally created and built Kubernetes, also known as K8s (after its eleven-letter abbreviation). After Kubernetes was made available to the public by Google in 2014, the Cloud Native Computing Foundation (CNCF) has been leading its development, with numerous people and organizations from across the world contributing. Kubernetes, backed by a robust ecosystem and used by both IT giants and startups, has quickly become the real standard for container orchestration.

Fundamentally, Kubernetes provides a platform for automating containerized application deployment, scaling, and management. Developers and operations teams may now think in terms of pods, services, and deployments rather than individual machines and their unique configurations because it abstracts the underlying infrastructure. In addition to streamlining operations, this abstraction guarantees a consistent environment for applications, regardless of the location of Kubernetes installation—on-site data centers, public clouds, or even a developer's desktop.

'Pod' refers to one or more containers that are deployed together on similar host and share the same network namespace. It is a basic notion in Kubernetes. Pods function as Kubernetes' atomic deployment unit, enabling closely connected application components to be co-located and communicate effectively, whereas Docker containers package the program and its dependencies. Every pod receives an IP address, which facilitates networking between them and guarantees fault tolerance and easy scaling.

Stable endpoints for pods are provided by services in Kubernetes. Services make sure that there's a consistent way to access the application by load-balancing traffic across available pods because pods are transient and can be terminated or spawned anytime based on scaling requirements or failures. The availability and robustness of applications depend heavily on this abstraction, particularly in dynamic situations where change is the only constant.

'Declarative configuration' is another idea that Kubernetes introduces. With Kubernetes, you declare the desired state for your application and the system makes sure that it is attained and maintained, eliminating the need to script the actions necessary to reach a specific state. An analogy for this would be adjusting the temperature on a thermostat: you select the desired temperature, and the system regulates the heating and cooling to make sure it is attained and maintained. You may specify how many instances of an application you want to run in Kubernetes, as well as which containers to use, how to network and store them, and Kubernetes takes care of the heavy lifting to make sure these requirements are met.

Kubernetes has built-in auto-scaling techniques to help with scalability. Kubernetes may autonomously spin up or tear down pod instances based on CPU use or other specific criteria, ensuring that applications can manage incoming traffic gracefully and without human intervention. Businesses that encounter fluctuating loads need this dynamic scaling capabilities in order to maximize expenses and resource use.

Aside from resilience, another feature of Kubernetes is self-healing. The system can automatically redistribute the load, launch new pods, and make sure the defined state is continually maintained in the event that nodes or pods fail. By lowering the need for manual monitoring and intervention, this method assures high availability and minimizes the possibility of downtime.

Another issue that Kubernetes skillfully handles is storage. In order to accommodate a variety of storage backends and requirements, Kubernetes offers Persistent Volumes (PVs) and Persistent Volume

Claims (PVCs), which abstract storage resources. This way, developers may request storage without having to worry about the specifics of local or cloud storage.

However, Kubernetes is a whole ecosystem, not just an orchestration platform. It provides native support for service discovery, monitoring, logging, and more, as well as extensions for many other features, thanks to its extensible architecture and plethora of plugins and integrations. Package management is made easier by tools like Helm, which let developers create, set up, and update even the most intricate Kubernetes applications.

In conclusion, Kubernetes has revolutionized the deployment and management of contemporary applications. By emphasizing flexibility, automated scaling, self-healing, and declarative configurations, it offers a complete framework for executing containerized applications at large scale. Underpinning the future of scalable, robust, and efficient software delivery, Kubernetes is a key player as enterprises continue their journey towards cloud-native architectures and digital transformation.

## Why combine Kubernetes with Docker?

Within the software industry, the ongoing advancement of technology is propelled by the enduring necessity to resolve intricate issues. Docker and Kubernetes are two contemporary technological marvels that tackle major issues in the field of application development and deployment. While Kubernetes has emerged as the industry leader in container orchestration, Docker has transformed the idea of containerization. Even if each tool is strong on its own, when used in conjunction, they provide synergies that have radically altered how contemporary applications are created, implemented, and scaled. This section explores why, in the context of cloud-native computing, Kubernetes and Docker, when combined, have become an indispensable pair.

Understanding each tool's unique strengths is the first step. Container technology gained popularity due to Docker, which gave programmers a means to package dependencies and applications into standardized units known as containers. Because Docker containers enclose the environment required to run the program, they ensure consistency across all stages of development and deployment, eliminating the notorious "it works on my machine" issue. With the advent of Docker, environments that were lightweight, isolated, and repeatable could be quickly shared, set up, and expanded.

But as more companies started using Docker and the quantity of containers increased, a new set of difficulties emerged. How are thousands or perhaps hundreds of thousands of containers managed, scaled, and networked? How can one accept defeat with grace? What is an ideal way to distribute resources? Here's where Kubernetes comes into play. Kubernetes was created to automate the deployment, scaling, and management of containerized applications. It was inspired by Google's extensive experience with Borg. It offered techniques for auto-scaling, service discovery, and self-healing in addition to introducing abstractions like pods, services, and deployments.

Kubernetes and Docker together now feel like a logical progression. Despite being naturally container-agnostic, Docker is frequently used in conjunction with Kubernetes as the container runtime. The fusion of these two technologies is advantageous and mutually reinforcing for the following reasons:

To begin with, Kubernetes scales up the management of these containers, while Docker supplies the standard container format. While Kubernetes guarantees that applications are always available, resilient, and scalable in response to demand, Docker guarantees that applications operate consistently in a variety of contexts. Using measurements like CPU usage, Kubernetes can scale in or out of Docker containers, check their health, and deploy them throughout a cluster of servers.

Furthermore, Docker's consistency is enhanced by Kubernetes' declarative approach to application management. Using Kubernetes manifests, developers can indicate the desired state of an application, including networking settings, the number of replicas to be used, and which Docker images to utilize. In order to keep things in this desired state, Kubernetes constantly deploys Docker containers when necessary and modifies resources to conform to the declaration.

Another area where the combination excels is networking. Docker ensures applications don't interact with one another by offering segregated networking for individual containers. By overseeing the networking of clusters of containers, or pods, and making sure they can interact with one another and the outside world, Kubernetes goes one step further in this regard. It manages DNS resolution, load balancing, and service discovery, which facilitates the operation of Docker containers as components of a larger, networked system.

Stateful applications require persistent storage, which Kubernetes elegantly manages with Docker containers. Docker volumes are somewhat ephemeral, particularly when they are replaced or moved. By introducing ideas like Persistent Volumes (PVs) and Persistent Volume Claims (PVCs), Kubernetes makes it possible for Docker containers to access reliable storage while hiding the intricacies of the underlying storage backend.

Furthermore, Kubernetes expands the resource efficiency benefits of Docker. Although Docker containers are less complex than virtual machines (VMs), Kubernetes makes sure that the most efficient use of resources is achieved by scheduling containers in an intelligent manner according to resource limits and requirements. It has the ability to effectively pack containers onto nodes, resulting in the least amount of CPU and memory waste.

Lastly, the robust ecosystem that has developed around Kubernetes and Docker is evidence of their synergy. Developers and operations teams can now build, deploy, monitor, and scale applications with simplicity and confidence due to tools for security, logging, monitoring, and CI/CD that have been developed with connectors for both Docker and Kubernetes.

In conclusion, while impressive on their own, Docker and Kubernetes work incredibly well together. With Kubernetes' strong orchestration capabilities complemented by Docker's lightweight and consistent containerization, enterprises have a strong platform to develop, launch, and administer contemporary cloud-native applications. In addition to accelerating the adoption of containers, this synergy has opened the door for a software delivery paradigm that is more scalable, resilient, and effective. The future of technology will surely be greatly influenced by the combined power of Kubernetes and Docker, as the wave of digital transformation continues to sweep all industries.

## Setting up a basic Kubernetes cluster with Docker

Within the ever-evolving field of cloud-native technologies, Kubernetes and Docker have become a well-known team for application orchestration and containerization. Industry-standard Docker container runtime is used in conjunction with powerful container orchestration platform Kubernetes, often known as K8s. When combined, they provide a smooth and comprehensive way to run containerized applications on many machine clusters. It may appear difficult for developers and operations staff who are unfamiliar with this field to put up a simple Kubernetes cluster powered by Docker. But it may be a simple and illuminating experience given the correct direction and comprehension. Using Docker as the container runtime, this section attempts to guide readers through the process of setting up a basic Kubernetes cluster.

Understanding the fundamental components of Kubernetes is necessary before beginning the setup procedure. Usually, a control plane and one or more worker nodes make up a basic Kubernetes cluster. The cluster management components, namely kube-apiserver, etcd, kube-scheduler, and kube-controller-manager, are hosted on the control plane. On the other hand, worker nodes, which also include the kubelet and kube-proxy components, run applications inside of containers. Within this design, Docker serves as the worker nodes' container runtime, managing the application containers.

Now, to the core of the setup process:

### 1. Preparing the Environment:

First and foremost, it is imperative to confirm that the machine—be it a server or a local workstation—satisfies the required specifications. This would entail having a Linux-based operating system (Windows and MacOS can function with extra tools), a hypervisor if utilizing minikube, and adequate CPU, memory, and storage resources for Kubernetes with Docker. Docker should also be installed on the workstation because our Kubernetes cluster will use it as its container runtime.

### 2. Kubernetes Tool Installation:

Installation of kubectl and a local cluster solution are prerequisites. The command-line tool for communicating with a Kubernetes cluster is called kubectl. Installing it can be done through the Kubernetes releases page binary download or using package managers such as apt or yum. While there are a number of possibilities for the local cluster, minikube stands out as a great option for novices because of its simplicity. Using a package management or downloading a binary can often be the easiest way to install minikube.

### 3. Cluster Launching:

It's quite easy to get the Kubernetes cluster up and running once the necessary tools are in place. A single-node Kubernetes cluster is established with the command minikube start --driver=<driver_name>, where the driver name refers to the hypervisor or Docker itself. Kubernetes executes containers directly within the Docker daemon without the need for a virtual machine when Docker is used as the driver, a setup known as Docker mode.

### 4. Verifying the Setup:

It's a good idea to confirm that everything is operating as it should after starting the cluster. Upon running the command kubectl get nodes, the minikube node with the state 'Ready' ought to appear. Furthermore, minikube status might offer more specific details regarding the health of the cluster. Running a test container might also help to make sure Docker and Kubernetes are properly integrating. This can be done using a simple deployment command, like kubectl create deployment nginx --image=nginx, followed by kubectl get pods to check the status of the deployed container.

### 5. Examining Basic Operations:

Now that the cluster is operational, it's a good idea to familiarize yourself with some basic Kubernetes functions. This can involve exposing a deployment as a service, adjusting the number of replicas for a deployment, reviewing logs, and providing pod data. The kubectl command is used in all of these activities, making it a vital tool for any Kubernetes practitioner.

### 6. Tearing Down and Cleaning Up:

It's important to know how to effectively tear down the cluster and clean up resources if you plan to use this setup as a learning or testing environment. While minikube delete thoroughly eliminates the cluster, minikube stop gently shuts it down. It makes sure that there are no configurations or residual components that could cause problems for upcoming setups or waste resources.

In conclusion, the procedure for establishing a basic Kubernetes cluster using Docker is a well-organized journey that provides priceless insights into the realm of container orchestration. The procedures mentioned above create the foundation for more intricate, multi-node configurations appropriate for production settings, even while they offer a straightforward single-node cluster good for learning and experimentation. Working with Kubernetes and Docker, even at a basic level, gives professionals the skills and knowledge they need to negotiate the changing landscape of modern application development and deployment as more and more enterprises adopt cloud-native technologies.

# CHAPTER XII

# Case Studies

## Real-world examples of companies using Docker

Since its launch, Docker has expanded quickly in the software development community's acceptability and appeal, and many businesses all over the world have integrated it into their processes. Developing the ability to encapsulate applications into containers has proven to be a game-changer for this containerization technology. This makes deployment, scalability, and operations simpler by guaranteeing a consistent environment wherever the container is run. A number of well-known businesses have integrated Docker into their development and production environments, which has helped them provide their customers with dependable, scalable, and effective services.

The well-known music streaming business Spotify was among the first and most notable users of Docker. With millions of active users, Spotify needs a smooth and effective infrastructure to guarantee continuous operation. For software deployment, Spotify used a mix of in-house scripts and Debian packages prior to Docker. However, this got cumbersome as their user base increased. Spotify improved their deployment process by switching to Docker. Spotify developers use Docker containers to encapsulate services, which are subsequently executed on a large number of servers. This guarantees a constant environment and performance, irrespective of the server's real setup. Spotify was also able to swiftly grow its services in response to variations in customer demand due to Docker's efficient orchestration.

PayPal is one of the major Docker users. The massive financial IT company was having trouble maintaining uniformity in the testing, production, and development environments. It was an enormous challenge to maintain environment consistency with over 700 applications and numerous development teams spread out throughout the globe. Docker offered an answer. PayPal was able to maintain consistency in the application's environment across development, production, and test servers by utilizing Docker containers. The development-to-deployment pipeline became more streamlined and effective as a result of the significant decrease in "it works on my machine" issues. Additionally, it allowed PayPal to run several containers on a single virtual machine (VM), which cut expenses and improved resource efficiency while optimizing infrastructure use.

Docker has proven to be a huge advantage for MetLife, a global supplier of insurance, annuities, and employee benefit programs. Because of its extensive history and multiple acquisitions, MetLife manages a wide range of legacy systems and applications. It was a difficult task to integrate these systems and make sure they communicated effectively. By encapsulating every legacy system inside containers, Docker came to the rescue and made the systems more manageable and modular. MetLife was able to save time and money by updating its infrastructure without having to replace or rewrite any of its outdated systems.

Leading newspaper and media outlet The New York Times has also used Docker as part of its digital transformation. The New York Times needed a method to effectively manage and distribute their digital assets, such as web pages and multimedia content, because of their constantly expanding digital readership. Docker enabled their developers to package services and applications, guaranteeing scalability and consistency. This was especially helpful when they started a drive to digitize and make their extensive collection of news articles—which spans more than a century—available. This enormous project was made easier for developers to work on different project components at the same time by Docker's agility.

Finally, Docker was used by ADP, a leading global provider of HRM solutions, to transform its application development and deployment procedures. With so many services it offers, including benefits administration and payroll, ADP needs a strong and flexible infrastructure. Because of Docker's containerization capabilities, ADP was able to create microservices, which are autonomous, small applications that can be independently scaled and deployed. Docker enabled this microservice design, which gave ADP more scalability, robustness, and agility.

In conclusion, the core of the IT infrastructures of numerous businesses now incorporates Docker's ground-breaking approach to containerization. Scalability, stability, and efficiency are three things that Docker has continuously delivered on, from financial huge companies like PayPal to music streaming services like Spotify. Its widespread use in a variety of industries attests to its adaptability and usefulness in addressing actual software development and deployment issues. In the digital age, platforms such as Docker will surely be crucial in determining how technology and service delivery develop and change in the future.

## Success stories and lessons learned

The environment for developing and deploying software has drastically changed thanks to Docker, an open-source containerization technology. Many enterprises have taken advantage of Docker's capabilities in the last few years, and they have reaped many benefits in terms of consistency, efficiency, and scalability. The triumphant narratives of these establishments encompass not only the advantages they procured, but also the knowledge they acquired, which provides invaluable perspectives for others wishing to initiate their Docker expedition.

General Electric (GE) is one of the most impressive success stories. With a wide range of industries under its purview, including healthcare and aviation, GE faced the enormous challenge of maintaining software consistency across several businesses. GE successfully standardized their software environment by including Docker into their development processes, which made it possible for developers from different industries to work together more effectively. The importance of establishing a centralized, corporate-wide Docker infrastructure was the main lesson GE took away from its Docker adventure. A cohesive strategy promoted cross-sector collaboration, knowledge sharing, and optimal resource allocation, as opposed to isolated teams working on Docker in silos.

Another well-known news organization in the world, BBC News, has effectively included Docker into its operations. They wanted to find an effective and reliable method of delivering material to a global audience. By enabling the creation of containerized microservices for content delivery, Docker offered a solution. They were able to accomplish quicker deployment timeframes, lower server costs, and improve content delivery consistency as a result. The BBC's experience served as a reminder of the value of ongoing observation and input. They were able to optimize performance by fine-tuning their Docker deployment by closely monitoring container performance and getting input from developers and end users.

Leading European financial services group Société Générale is another noteworthy success story. Their software development process needed more agility and speed, so they turned to Docker for it in order to stay up with the constantly changing finance industry. By moving to a containerized environment, Société Générale was able to shorten the time it takes for new financial products and services to hit the market by speeding up its software release cycle. Their experience at Docker shed light on the value of making training and skill development investments. Several development teams had trouble at first adjusting to the Docker environment. But by making a significant investment in thorough Docker training courses, they made sure that their staff members were prepared to fully utilize the platform.

Renowned university Cornell University provides a distinct academic success story about Docker. Cornell turned to Docker when faced with the difficulty of delivering uniform software environments for students in different courses. They made sure all students had access to a standardized software environment regardless of how their personal computers were configured by containerizing software programs. This lowered the administrative burden for IT teams in addition to leveling the playing field for students. Docker's transformational power extends beyond the corporate realm, as demonstrated by Cornell's experience. Institutions can utilize Docker's capabilities in a variety of creative and inventive ways by thinking beyond the box.

These accomplishments highlight Docker's enormous potential, but they also highlight the difficulties that enterprises encountered. One theme that runs across all of these tales is how crucial cooperation and communication are. The implementation of Docker frequently requires a change in the way development teams work. Maintaining open lines of communication among teams is essential for resolving issues and maximizing the use of Docker.

The importance of thorough testing is yet another crucial lesson. Docker promises consistency, but when programs are containerized, their unique characteristics can occasionally lead to unexpected behavior. It is imperative to conduct routine testing in both development and production settings in order to detect and resolve possible problems.

Moreover, Docker is not a panacea, even though it streamlines a lot of software development processes. Businesses now understand how important it is to specify the goals and parameters of their Docker adoption. If Docker is used merely to follow the trend without considering its applicability and possible advantages for the company, it may not work as well as it could.

In conclusion, Docker has unquestionably had a significant influence on the software development industry. Success stories from various organizations, including academic institutions and media behemoths, demonstrate to its adaptability and revolutionary impact. Nonetheless, there are obstacles in the way of Docker's progress. Organizations may make better navigational decisions during their Docker journey and ensure that they fully utilize Docker to accomplish their specific goals by examining the lessons gained from early adopters. The experiences of these innovators provide insightful perspectives that will influence the direction of containerized software development as Docker continues to expand.

## Challenges faced and how Docker provided solutions

Businesses and developers alike encounter several obstacles in today's fast-paced technology ecosystem when attempting to build, scale, and sustain applications. A significant solution to many of these problems has been revealed in the form of Docker, a groundbreaking containerization platform. However, in order to fully recognize Docker's disruptive potential, one must comprehend the particular issues it solves and the creative solutions it presents.

In software development, one of the biggest obstacles is the "It works on my machine" mentality. Frequently, developers discover that an application that functions perfectly on their local computer develops errors or stops working altogether when it is implemented in a different setting. The differences between development, staging, and production environments' software versions, configurations, or underlying system dependencies are usually to blame for this. Docker encapsulates applications and their dependencies into containers, offering a solution to this widespread issue. Because these containers don't care about the environment, the application will function reliably at every step of the development process, from the local setup of a developer to the production server. This uniform setting eliminates the disparities that result in unexpected errors and minimizes the duration required for troubleshooting environment-specific problems.

The inefficiency of resources is a major problem for businesses. Conventional virtualization techniques, such as the use of Virtual Machines (VMs), use hypervisors—each running a complete operating system—to divide the underlying hardware. This causes a large amount of overhead because each virtual machine uses a substantial amount of system resources. Docker's approach to lightweight containerization mitigates this issue. All Docker containers run in separate user areas and share the same OS kernel, as opposed to running different operating systems. Because of this architectural distinction, containers use considerably less resources than virtual machines. With the ability to run several containers on a single server, businesses may maximize resource consumption and cut expenses associated with infrastructure.

Businesses frequently have trouble scaling their applications to accommodate rising user demand as they expand. Rapid service scalability might be hampered by the slow and laborious nature of traditional deployment techniques. Docker's containerized applications provide an answer to this issue. Horizontal scalability can happen quickly thanks to containers' speedy instantiation. Additionally, companies may automate the scaling process based on real-time demand with orchestration solutions like Kubernetes or Docker Swarm, guaranteeing that they can manage traffic spikes without the need for manual intervention.

Another issue that many well-established businesses deal with is the integration of outdated technologies. Despite being essential to corporate operations, these older systems frequently use outdated software stacks, which makes it challenging to connect them with more recent programs. Here, Docker provides a lifeline by enabling enterprises to containerize their legacy applications. By 'wrapping' the outdated software in a more contemporary, standardized environment, containerization improves compatibility with existing systems and reduces integration difficulties.

Software deployment has always been dominated by security issues. It is crucial to make sure that applications are isolated from one another and the underlying system. In conventional configurations, other applications that are operating on the same system may be compromised by a security flaw in one of the applications. This issue is resolved by Docker containers, which offer a robust isolation border. Every container communicates with its own isolated user space, maintaining the separation of programs. Because of this segregation, the possible impact of security breaches is reduced because invasions are kept within the compromised container and do not spread to other containers.

And last, there's the issue of software rollbacks and updates. Businesses must regularly update their applications in dynamic markets in order to either provide new features or fix security flaws. But it might be difficult to make sure upgrades go smoothly without bringing down the system or creating faults. Docker's immutable infrastructure concept offers a solution to this issue. Docker advocates for the development of new containers with updated software rather than updating existing ones. With minimal downtime, these containers can then be effortlessly replaced with the previous ones. Businesses can also promptly rollback by restoring the prior container if problems occur with the new upgrade, guaranteeing service continuity.

In conclusion, the various difficulties that developers and companies encounter in the deployment and maintenance of software are the reason behind Docker's ascent in the technological world. With its ability to address issues with resource inefficiencies, scaling, legacy system integration, security, and update complexity, Docker has solidified its place as a vital tool in modern software operations. With Docker's revolutionary approach to containerization, businesses can survive in the ever-evolving digital landscape by having the robustness, flexibility, and efficiency they need.

# CONCLUSION

## The future of Docker and containerization

A paradigm shift in software development and deployment has been heralded by Docker and containerization. These tools have improved consistency across environments, expedited processes, and given application deployment greater agility. However, Docker and containerization are merely steps in a constantly changing path, much like other technology developments. It's critical to take into account the potential directions, technological advancements, and difficulties that Docker and the larger containerization landscape may face as we move forward.

Technology's constant quest of optimization is at its core, and Docker is no different. We may anticipate that Docker will get increasingly more resource-efficient as time goes on. Although they operate in isolated user areas, current containers use the same OS kernel. Still, additional research into microVMs—small, light virtual machines—could improve this concept even more by combining the greatest aspects of containers and virtual machines. Combining these two technologies could give an extra degree of security without compromising the speed and effectiveness that containers are known for.

Cross-platform capabilities will probably be another area of progress. Even while Docker has made progress in providing solutions for a range of platforms, there is a growing need for containers to function flawlessly on a variety of architectures, such as x86, ARM, and others. Having more and more devices, from edge devices to mainframes, will fracture our digital environment, making truly platform-agnostic containers more and more necessary. In order to meet this need, Docker and other industry participants will be at the forefront of developing their tools and offering a unified containerization experience.

Security has always been the top priority and always will be. Malicious actors find Docker and container technologies increasingly appealing as they grow more ingrained in enterprise contexts. We can expect Docker to make significant investments to strengthen the security aspects of containers in anticipation of this. Crucial areas of attention will be closer interaction with enterprise security solutions, extensive vulnerability scanning, and enhanced runtime defenses. Additionally, it will be crucial to make sure that containerized applications follow these standards as laws pertaining to data security and privacy become more stringent.

More advanced container orchestration is also something that seems promising for the future. Although Kubernetes and other tools have made great progress in managing and scaling containers, innovation is still possible. The complexity of microservices architectures and the explosion of deployed containers will require orchestration technologies to advance in intelligence. Future orchestration systems may use AI and machine learning to detect and fix problems in containers autonomously, optimize resource allocation in real-time, and anticipate scalability requirements based on traffic trends.

The possible integration of Docker with cutting-edge technologies like quantum computing is an intriguing but more theoretical avenue for its future development. Software paradigms that support quantum computers will need to change as these machines get closer to being useful in real-world applications. Because of its emphasis on environment consistency, Docker may be essential in establishing standardized settings for quantum processing, guaranteeing that quantum software is consistent with both conventional and quantum hardware.

But there are obstacles in the way of this voyage. The swift expansion of containerization and microservices also raises difficult issues. It becomes increasingly difficult to manage inter-container relationships, ensure data consistency, and monitor these huge ecosystems as enterprises deploy hundreds or thousands of containers. It will be necessary for Docker versions to come up with tools and paradigms in the future to make these intricacies simpler and prevent the very solutions designed to speed up development from becoming cumbersome.

Additionally, because technology is cyclical, it is always possible for newer paradigms to arise and render the ones that already exist outdated. Even with their current prominence, containerization and Docker are not immune to this cycle. It's possible that whole new approaches to software deployment and administration will emerge in the future, making containerization a footnote to the history of technology. Docker will have to constantly innovate, adjust, and maybe even reimagine its basic values in order to be relevant.

In conclusion, there is a lot of potential, complex difficulties, and unavoidable evolution ahead for Docker and containerization. These tools will evolve along with the software landscape, meeting the ever-changing demands of organizations, developers, and emerging technologies. Even if it's hard to foresee the future with absolute confidence, one thing is certain: Docker and containerization are significant forces that will both shape and be shaped by the technological paradigm of the years to come, not merely trends in technology.

## Resources for further learning and exploration

Docker is a remarkable tool in the constantly changing world of software development and deployment because it has revolutionized the methods for containerizing, deploying, and scaling applications. Like any major technological breakthrough, learning Docker takes commitment, practice, and access to high-quality learning materials. Many forms and levels of information are available for individuals who want to learn more about Docker or for seasoned pros who want to improve their skills.

Books have always been considered to be the most complete sources of information, and there are a few that are particularly noteworthy regarding Docker. Nigel Poulton's "Docker Deep Dive" offers a thorough analysis of Docker, making sure that readers comprehend not just its features but also its fundamental ideas. For individuals who are particularly interested in incorporating Docker into the broader DevOps environment, James Turnbull's "The Docker Book: Containerization is the new virtualization" provides useful advice and interactive activities. For those who want to learn Docker's nuances in-depth, books are a great resource due to their well-organized format and comprehensive material.

Due to their ease and participatory nature, online courses have become increasingly popular. There are other Docker courses available on sites like Pluralsight, Coursera, and Udemy, each suited for a different degree of experience. Courses such as "Docker and Kubernetes: The Complete Guide" available on Udemy provide a strong foundation for novices by explaining fundamental ideas and offering practical assignments. More experienced users may choose to enroll in specialist courses covering orchestration, security best practices, or even Docker's interaction with particular tools. Because online courses are active and frequently include forums or Q&A sessions, learners are guaranteed to obtain both academic information and practical guidance.

An often-underappreciated informational gold mine is Docker's official documentation. It offers comprehensive instructions on all facets of Docker, ranging from setup to sophisticated applications. The documentation is kept up to date with the most recent Docker releases through careful maintenance. It is also user-friendly in structure, making it suitable for both beginners and professionals. Stack Overflow and the official Docker forums offer a wealth of debates and answers to frequent (and rare) problems faced by Docker users worldwide, for those who prefer a more problem-solving approach.

Conferences and workshops offer yet another way to explore Docker. Occurring events such as DockerCon provide networking opportunities in addition to various educational programs. Direct interaction with Docker enthusiasts, professionals, and peers in the field offers a comprehensive learning experience that combines academic knowledge with real-world applications and practical insights. Moreover, a lot of these events include practical workshops that let participants put what they've learned to use right away, which promotes retention and better understanding.

Podcasts about containerization and Docker provide an alternative learning format for those who are auditory learners. Podcasts such as "PodCTL" and "The New Stack Analysts" usually cover Docker, its ecosystem, and the implications that it has for the industry. These podcasts give listeners a combination of technical knowledge, industry trends, and expert perspectives. They frequently feature interviews with industry professionals.

Open-source learning communities such as GitHub host a multitude of Docker-related projects, tools, and resources in this era of community-driven learning. Investigating these archives has two advantages. First of all, it provides a useful understanding of how Docker is applied in actual projects. Second, people can improve their Docker abilities and contribute back to the community at the same time by actively contributing to these repositories.

Lastly, for individuals who prefer a structured, long-term approach, multiple institutions and training centers offer certification programs in Docker. One such acknowledged certification that assesses a candidate's proficiency in a variety of Docker-related areas is the Docker Certified Associate (DCA). Getting ready for these certifications offers a well-organized study path and results in an acknowledged qualification that can elevate one's career status.

In conclusion, there are a plethora of materials available to support various styles of learning and technical proficiency levels along the path to becoming a Docker expert. Books, courses, documentation, forums, events, podcasts, open-source projects, and certifications are all available in the Docker learning ecosystem to help you along the way, regardless of your level of experience. Using these tools in conjunction with regular practice and practical application guarantees that those who are interested can fully utilize Docker's capabilities and stay at the forefront of this revolutionary technology movement.

*Thank you for buying and reading/listening to our book. If you found this book useful/helpful please take a few minutes and leave a review on the platform where you purchased our book. Your feedback matters greatly to us.*